Reading in the Sunshine,
Laughing Every Day

BOOKS BY SAM PICKERING

ESSAY COLLECTIONS

A Continuing Education

The Right Distance

May Days

Still Life

Let It Ride

Trespassing

The Blue Caterpillar

Living to Prowl

Deprived of Unhappiness

A Little Fling

The Last Book

The Best of Pickering

Indian Summer

Autumn Spring

Journeys

Dreamtime

The Splendour Falls

All My Days Are Saturdays

Happy Vagrancy

One Grand, Sweet Song

Parade's End

The World Was My Garden, Too

Terrible Sanity

The Gate In The Garden Wall

"The Truth"

TRAVEL

Walkabout Year

Waltzing the Magpies

Edinburgh Days

A Tramp's Wallet

LITERARY STUDIES

The Moral Tradition in English Fiction, 1785–1850

John Locke and Children's Books in Eighteenth-Century England

Moral Instruction and Fiction for Children, 1749–1820

TEACHING

Letters to a Teacher

MEMOIR

A Comfortable Boy

Reading in the Sunshine, Laughing Every Day

ESSAYS

Sam Pickering

MERCER UNIVERSITY PRESS

Macon, Georgia

MUP/ P723

Published by Mercer University Press
1501 Mercer University Drive
Macon, Georgia 31207

29 28 27 26 25 5 4 3 2 1

Books published by Mercer University Press are printed on acid-free paper that meets the requirements of the American National Standard for Information Sciences—Permanence of Paper for Printed Library Materials.

Printed and bound in the United States.

This book is set in Adobe Garamond .

Cover/jacket design by Burt&Burt.

ISBN 978-0-88146-983-7
Cataloging-in-Publication Data is available from the Library of Congress

Contents

MERCER
UNIVERSITY

MERCER UNIVERSITY PRESS

Endowed by

TOM WATSON BROWN
and
THE WATSON-BROWN FOUNDATION, INC.

Appreciation

Dedications are batters of sentences doused with artificial sweeteners. I've baked cookie trays of them. Their forced bonhomie has always made my pencil curdle, but because readers sampled them without suffering diabetic seizures, I continued cooking them. However, age changes people's tastes. It has changed mine. Now the thought of composing another dedication gives me diverticulitis. After thumbing several medical newsletters, I've concluded that the most effective contraceptive is an appreciation thickened with heads of bushy green verbs and topped with dollops of literary bran.

Margery Sharp's *The Nutmeg Tree* was published in 1937. Julia, the main character, was five feet three inches tall and 39 years old. She had a thirty-eight-inch bust, forty-one-inch hips, and a thirty-one-inch waist. "Three vital points," Sharp judged, "linked by extremely agreeable curves." At the beginning of the book Julia appeared lounging in a bathtub singing the "La Marseillaise." A rosy cloud of steam hovered over her, and she looked "like the presiding goddess of some baroque ceiling." The bathroom was locked, and while Julia sang, two bailiffs banged on the door. Piled around the tub were Julia's possessions, the jumbled contents of the garage sale into which all people's worldly goods eventually disappear: a coffee table, clothes, seven hat boxes, a mattress, half a dinner service, three suitcases, thirty-five novelettes, a small grandfather clock, and a print of one of Landseer's stags. Julia eventually escaped the bath by selling everything to the local pawnbroker, earning sixteen pounds, ten shillings, enough to pay five quid to the bailiffs and to purchase a ticket to France.

She traveled to France to monitor the love affair of her twenty-year-old daughter whom she had not seen in sixteen years. The girl lived with her grandmother. Julia hadn't known the girl's father well. "The first time Julia had seen her future husband by daylight," Sharp recounted, "was on a spring morning in 1916, when she woke at half-past ten to find him still sleeping by her side." He was an officer in the Gunners. On discovering that she was pregnant, Julia wrote him in France. After urging him "not to worry," she asked if he could "lend her a hand." In reply, she received the "shock of her life." He obtained a forty-eight-hour leave, returned to England, and married her. Two months later he was killed at Ypres, and Julia's daughter was born at Barton, the home of the Packetts, her new in-laws. The Packetts were affectionate and responsible. For a year and a half Julia was a dutiful daughter-in-law, but eventually the struggle to be good became too great and entrusting her little girl to the Packetts, left Barton and "went thoroughly back to the bad." Of course, Julia wasn't bad. She was joyous and warm-hearted, round-heeled and loving. She was spontaneous and irresponsible, if being responsible demands adherence to anesthetizing propriety. In truth Julia was more metaphor than person. She was life itself—life as it could be, and as it is sometimes embraced, and, of course, as it is often avoided.

Appreciation of Julia and of the rambunctious nature of life comes easier to the old than to the young. Age both enlightens and lightens as rails slip from the fences of schooled convention. Rarely does an oldster bolt the paddock in which he has lived for decades, but often he becomes more tolerant and appreciative of disorderly living. He remembers the past and savors the richness of both the good and the not-so-good. He will likely romanticize lost possibilities and missteps.

Harlequin days may intrigue him, and recollection may cause his heart to throb but not to ache. In *The Nutmeg Tree*, an older man appreciates Julia and becomes, if not her husband, at least her keeper, and treasurer.

To understand men, Julia decided, "to realize the full value of their good streaks, while pardoning the bad—you had to know so many of them." Many years enable a person to understand and to appreciate life with its good and bad streaks. Sharp's novel appeared four years before I was born. It and I are octogenarians. Vicki calls me "Mr. Geriatric." Last week as I waited for Vicki at the entrance to Price Chopper, a woman leaving the checkout and I noticed each other simultaneously. "I thought that was you," she said, pausing for a moment. "I thought that was you, too," I answered. "It is always good to see you," she said rolling her cart toward the parking lot. "It is always good to see you, too," I replied. "Is that all you both said?" Vicki asked. "Yes," I answered. "Who was she?" Vicki said. "I have no idea," I replied. "I couldn't remember her name. But that's all right. She was my age and couldn't remember my name either."

Yesterday I rinsed a handful of blueberries under a faucet in the kitchen sink. Unfortunately, I held the strainer wrong side up. Instead of shaking the berries into the wire cup, I dumped them atop the mesh. Almost before I noticed, they swished around the sink and dove into the garbage disposal. "Twenty-three berries," Vicki said later removing her hand from the disposal. "My dear," Vicki said, quoting the last line of *The Nutmeg Tree*, a question asked by Julia's older lover, "What on earth will you do next?" The things I'll do until Lethe sweeps me and my past and present away will be insignificant and often silly. They'll help me appreciate life and imagine luscious days of splashing about with Julia, listening to her “robust contralto,” bailiffs and pawnbrokers rattling the door, and the cluttering nothings of her life lapping over the lip of the tub. “Vicki,” I responded. “Didn’t you say that the bill for your plate and new tooth was five thousand dollars?” “Yes, the price was robbery,” Vicki answered. “I don’t know about criminality,” I said. “But I have done some gum-fund cost analysis. If you live ten more years, the price amortizes to five hundred dollars a year or nine dollars and sixty-two cents a week or one dollar and thirty-seven cents a day. To me that smacks of overbite and distasteful spendthrift behavior. But if you live twenty years, the cost is palatable at two hundred and fifty dollars a year, four dollars and eighty-one cents a week, and a solvent sixty-seven cents a day.” “Yes,” Vicki answered, “and a cash flow of only 2.8 cents an hour.”

Introduction

"Once upon a time," Anne Tyler began *Back When We Were Grownups*, "there was a woman who discovered that she had turned into the wrong person." During their lives, individuals become many people, some of them right, some wrong. At least they do until no gold threads linger among the silver. Suppleness vanishes, and their minds and bodies harden into inflexibility. For two decades I declared that each new collection of my essays was my final book. For a week afterward the assertion was true, but then something quickened my interest, and I resumed writing. I didn't become another person. I only changed direction marginally and beat a slightly different trail through signatures of pages.

In *The Old Ways: A Journey on Foot*, Robert Macfarlane said that "paths are the habits of a landscape." For me, habits of living make paths, and lives shape landscapes, not landscapes lives. This introduction is a path, a familiar way, not a track crossing the unfamiliar and marked by the startling: healing wells, anchor holds, and stiletto-like hoodoos. I have walked the way backward and forward so often that the path has sunk deep into my writing and become a narrative holloway. Certainly, I occasionally strayed and explored wayside scrub. Additionally, Time tripped me, and I tottered into a different perspective. Yet the landscape rising above the path hasn't changed much recently. Indeed, it appears hardened, the particulars confining the holloway molded and baked by repetitive living.

I cannot remember when I wasn't a reader, and in my essays, I refer to innumerable books, many of the volumes deservedly forgotten, momentarily, and only momentarily, resuscitated by being hauled out of discard bins. Regrettably, I left the actual classroom twelve years ago. I "loved" teaching, and when I stumble upon a school novel, I read it, no matter its literary quality. Last month I read Latta Griswold's *Deering of Deal or The Spirit of the School* published in 1912. In a melancholy mood, Morris, a popular master, wondered if he'd wasted "his life in the obscurity of a petty profession," neglecting "the talents, abilities, ambitions, that in college days had promised a brilliant career." Morris's gloom lifted on his concluding that "the response he got from the stimulus he gave to boys" was recompence. Brilliance is generally fictional while recompence often smacks of snake oil hawked by self-help gurus. Perhaps, I thought as I read the novel, people became schoolteachers in order to escape ulcerating talents and ambition and to live indulgently in accordance with their inclinations, not the demands of place or position. In the preface to *And Dogs To Chase Them*, Ray Trotter quoted what he said was a proverb among Southern lawyers, "the one who tells the best story wins." Morris ought to have admitted that teaching was simply teaching and that the best classrooms were anthologies, their contents bulging with suggestive fragments.

Bookish people are usually omnivores, besides reading paragraphs and chapters, noticing and remarking on the run-on scree of daily life. On my pages, among many others, the fragments consist of advertisements, slogans printed on T-shirts, and found papers, the last sometimes homemade bookmarks, grocery lists, or simply puzzling remnants. Woven into my essays and supporting the banks along my path are miscellanies of writing. These are often small things. Yet they cause me to pause and seem significant although I can't explain why. Rather, I don't want to dizzy readers by forcing explanations and, in the process, losing control of my sentences and straying from the holloway. Every year, for example, Betsy sends me a calendar. Betsy is my age, and she and her husband Runo live on a farm in Michigan. They garden and raise sheep. For many days in her calendar, Betsy writes one or two sentences, very different from the entries listing doctors' appointments which Vicki records on our calendar. Last year on May 21, Betsy saw "the first bobolink." A month later "the first lightning bugs" appeared. On the twelfth of September, Betsy wrote, "we sorted lambs yesterday and today sent 133 to the lamb pool auction. Later, went to the garden and picked three pints of fall raspberries and several pails of tomatoes." Eleven days afterward, "Runo picked the Liberty apples and the first from the Cox Orange Pippin tree. The Golden Russets will be on the tree for some time yet." On the first of December, the temperature was twenty-two degrees Fahrenheit, and "We rendered lard today. Ten quarts of pure white lard now in the freezer."

How much more comfortable and thought-provoking, perhaps poetic, to know that on a rainy day early in January "Runo manned the carding machine" and Betsy "worked at the spinning wheel" rather than that I walked downtown to see a "new" cardiologist. In the waiting room, a friend and I discussed dementia. A man eavesdropped on our conversation. After my friend left, the man addressed me, meaning to be reassuring. "I know all about dementia. There's been a lot in my family," he said. "You shouldn't worry much about it now. It's hardly noticeable. Everybody forgets names like your friend said." The man then asked my age. On my telling him 82, he said his grandmother had dementia for fifteen or sixteen years. "She lived to 96, and until she was ninety my wife and I took care of her. After she reached ninety, we couldn't manage without the help of daycare and a visiting nurse." As for my heart, it was ambling along at a carefree 39 beats a minute, my pulse practically whistling "zip-a-dee-doo-dah."

Happenstance shapes most of my days and pages. Generally, my past dozes soundly, but then occasionally a letter or a remark awakens a memory. Recently, a childhood friend asked what I thought about the hullabaloo over sex education in public schools, testifying that he'd come by such knowledge naturally when he visited an uncle's farm during summer vacations. His statement awakened recollections of my working in an automotive supply store. At the time I was a new teenager. Although I could waltz gracefully through all Nine Circles of Society, I knew little about fleshly matters. On discovering my ignorance, my older fellow workers Doug Little and Otis Rutherford educated me. With an occasional lesson plan given to them by a driver named Bo but popularly known as Ob, they crafted fanciful descriptions of anatomy highlighted by exotic male and female doings. Their accounts entertained and smacked of fairy tales. They untethered my imagination and awakened curiosity. How fortunate I was that school didn't teach sex education. How lucky that a teacher did not lift the hood of unknowing and undermined daydreaming by exposing private matters, reducing them to mechanics, showing them to be composed of carburetors, air filters, and heat pumps, crank shafts and grommets. All that came much later, a repetitive "all that," to draw from Robert Graves, to which saying good-bye became darn near impossible.

Individual pieces in collections of personal essays can be the equivalents of chapters, and if so inclined, an intent reader might discover or impose a tale. I don't tell stories to win, but like the ingredients of fruit cakes, anecdotes layer my pages. As should be expected of a final book, more are medical than candied or alcoholic although examining-room happenings are sometimes nutty and intoxicating. Recently, as a young nurse's aide took my blood pressure, I noticed a small heart tattooed on her left arm. The heart was not a Valentine's Day cartoon. It was a replica of the human heart. Arteries stuck up like udders out of the aorta, and the right and left atriums bulged rumpled like walnut shells. However, a channel looking like a miniature lightning bolt ran searing down the middle of the heart dividing it into halves. "I know my blood pressure is all right," I said to the aide, "but tell me about the heart on your arm." "I got it when my husband ran off with another woman and divorced me," the aide replied. "Oh, dear," I said. "I hope you don't have to have more hearts tattooed on your arm." "Me, too, when I was first married, I never imagined getting this," the aide said, turning her head aside and brushing a tear off her cheek.

Because the incurable drapes over my remaining academic friends, shapeless and unwashed like an ancient sweater pulled from the bottom of a sugar chest, I don't write as much about clinical doings as I once did. Moreover, Vicki's attitude toward medical matters, especially mine, has darkened. A fortnight ago, she asked, "What will I do after you die?" Still, high times haven't completely disappeared from doctors' offices. At Vicki's insistence in November, a doctor gouged a lipoma out of my arm. I called the lump a peanut. "Peanut!" the doctor exclaimed, "It was ginormous, the largest lipoma I've removed." The incision was longer than six inches. Later the doctor trenched it to drain fluid that had clumped in marble-sized seromas, or "gunkles," as Vicki labeled them. I mailed a picture of the trench to several elementary school companions. Atop the paper I wrote the header "Eat Your Heart Out." The gay days when first graders eagerly exhibited scars and scabs, always insisting on charging a penny, were over. None of the "boys" to whom I sent the photograph replied. Alas, Time changes everything. Even funerals aren't fun nowadays. Unlike corpses dressed and waxed for the underground strutters' ball, ashes don't elicit ribald memories and fond, inappropriate comments.

Sixty-two years ago, I spent six weeks by myself rambling behind the Iron Curtain. I had little money, and I cadged reduced rates in hotels and on trains by saying I was a young American communist. While "yellow leaves or none" now adorn my boughs, my bank account has rooted and grown suckers. I don't own an orchard laden with ripening greenbacks, but instead of finagling, I can afford to pay stated prices. Fortunately, and unfortunately, travel has become more comfortable and lost most of its romance. Places over the hills and damn far away that I visited and once dreamed of visiting have been demystified. Nevertheless, I still traipse about. Fooling myself into fancying I'm roaming beyond the mundane, I write about my travels. Still, it is dispiriting to go to a once exotic place and after returning home discover hordes of people have recently been there. Even worse they behave apishly and photograph themselves grinning and screeching, waving their hands, and waggling their tongues, backsides, and sometimes bare chests. Under the pictures, they write comments. Many consist of a single word, "awesome," "wow," "cool," and

"OMG" being popular. A goodly number of such tourists conclude their commentaries with gameday gridiron chants, a preponderance of these being zoological, among others, "Go Bears," "Wooo Pig Sooie—Razor Backs," "Hook'em Horns," "War Eagle," "Go Terps," "On You Gophers," and on the page celebrating the Taste of Jamaica Farm Cookout, "Bulldog. Bulldog. Bow Wow Wow."

For forty years I described summers Vicki and I, and our children, spent in rural Nova Scotia in Four Winds, an old house her father bought in 1947. Recently I have written extensively about Four Winds. The reason is paradoxical. Less has provoked more. Vicki and I have witnessed, and felt, a great diminution. Gone are the moths that blanketed our screen door at night. Gone are the butterflies that blew like confetti over our fields. Gone are the shorebirds and the flocks of warblers that swept through the wood in September. Yes, living shaped my holloway, but the landscape also molded me. In essays I write about abundance and what I wish were still abundant. The effects of the industrial Anthropocene are visible everywhere. Not long ago my town adopted the motto, "Your Place to Grow." And grown Mansfield has, accompanied by the music of chain saws and bulldozers. My friend Josh says the motto ought to be "Your Place to Enjoy a Traffic Jam." Marching to the same machinery is the university. It chops and uproots, constructs Brutalist buildings, and increases enrollment to the thump of branding and self-congratulatory propaganda.

Streets in Mansfield have become slaughterhouses. On days when a basketball team performs, drivers become knackers. Deer no longer bed down amid leaves in the wood behind my house. Instead, they sleep on the shoulders of roads. Gone from my yard are the little folk—the groundhogs, raccoons, opossums, foxes, skunks, and flying squirrels, even the crows, that I saw every day, creatures that dissolved loneliness and taught that I belonged and was part of a great natural world. Unlike Morris in *Deering of Deal*, I don't believe that teaching, or in this case, writing, necessarily influences people for the better. But as an octogenarian I have lived long enough both to hope and to have given up hope. As a result, I seed essays with references to the natural. These are usually plants and animals that most readers haven't seen and probably will never see, recently, for example, a tiger grouper, its head measled with spots, spiders lurking behind nickel-sized trapdoors in a clay bank, white-tailed sabrewing hummingbirds so tame they perch on people's fingers and sip nectar from thumb-sized feeders, and then graying under trumpet trees, a panacea for bronchitis, dried round clusters of leaves, the tips of the leaflets rolling inward like the side curls that embellished eighteenth-century wigs. Maybe my mentioning unfamiliar things will awaken curiosity and, as it does for me, indirectly encourage readers not only to notice but also to appreciate their immediate surroundings. On returning to Storrs after a trip before Christmas, I became aware of sawtooth oaks for the first time. While many leaves remained on the oaks gleaming and crinkling in breezes, others had fallen and around the trunks wove caramel-colored mats, the teeth on the margins sharp yet lacy and delicate.

In this book, I cajole. Occasionally I preach, but rarely do I mount a bully pulpit. I cannot answer the questions Mary Oliver asks in "The Summer Day." "Who made the world? / Who made the swan, and the black bear? / Who made the grasshopper?" If I am awake at thirty-four minutes past midnight, I say loudly, "Attention. Attention. 1-2-3-4. 1-2-3-4" immediately followed by "Backward. Backward. 4-3-2-1. 4-3-2-1." After a minute passes, I say, "Over. Over." I've repeated this statement scores, no, years of times. I am not my own mystery. Yet I cannot explain why I began saying these words and numerals nor why I continue, indeed why I do and think many, many things. "I just does."

I write little about politics. Remedies for the cankers poisoning this country and the world, even definitions of the problems themselves are, as Peter, Paul, and Mary put it, "blowing in the wind"—a venomous, suppurating wind. I sit and write, metaphorically wielding a pencil filled with soft rather than hard lead. I describe, ponder, and celebrate. My holloway is worn. The end is in sight, and although from time to time I stagger, I generally keep on an almost straight, recognizable path. Last year, Josh asked what my subject was. "I've read most of your books," he said. "But I am not sure what's been your over-riding subject." "Life," Vicki told him. "Life as people live and don't live." Last Wednesday, Vicki and I went on a date. I drove six miles to Big Y grocery near Willimantic. Paczki season had arrived. In a shadowy nook behind and between the store's flower shop and bakery are six tables. Almost never are the tables occupied. On Wednesday I found a package of two paczkis, and Vicki bought coffee from a machine on the kitchen counter. Paczkis resemble jelly doughnuts and are round tubs of dough injected with jam-like fillings. Big Y sold four varieties, each containing a different filling, raspberry, lemon, apple, and prune.

As doxycycline mitigates the effects of Lyme disease, so paczkis counteract the unsociable consequences of addictions to dieting. For the record, or menu, Vicki and I are selective and only eat paczkis distended with prune fillings. "You and

Mom are living large. Gobs of prune in a doughnut," Edward said later, "A Fast Unplugging Sweet only appealing to the oldest of the old." Edward's judgment aside, Vicki and I had a marvelous date, sitting in the dim, indeed romantic, light, sharing a medium-sized paper cup of coffee, munching paczkis, and turning our fingers as sticky as adhesive tape, and, of course, studying and commenting on shoppers as they rolled by pushing carts. After finishing her paczki, Vicki said she needed exercise and disappeared down an aisle searching for "five or six items."

I felt torpid so I sat on the only bench in the store. The bench was in front of the checkout counters, and soon a woman joined me. She was my age and while she waited for a taxi, we chatted as strangers talk who know they won't see one another again. The woman had spent twenty years in Uganda and returned to Connecticut to care for an ailing mother. Although she was grasping the knob on death's door, the mother recovered and lived much longer. By the time her mother died, the woman herself was old. "I dreamed of returning to Uganda, but I wasn't carefree as I once was, and I couldn't muster the energy." For my part in the conversation, I told her about acquaintances who went to East Africa, one of whom died from AIDS and another who discovered a viper. We both talked about Time's passing, and things often thought about but not done. "Shaking loose from home," as Carl Hoffman phrased it in *The Lunatic Express*, his account of traveling on the world's most dangerous, buses, boats, trains, and planes.

If a person wanders a holloway, even though the track is so familiar he can walk it blindfolded, every day something will startle him. On standing to go to her taxi, the woman recited two lines from a poem I hadn't mentioned in our talk, but which I'd cited in a recent essay. "A health unto the happy!" she said. "A fig for him who frets!" "It isn't raining rain to me," I replied. "It's raining violets." "What a fortuitous conversation," the woman then said. "Yes, wasn't it?" I answered. While Vicki and I were on our date, the mail arrived at home. Among the letters was one from a high school companion. Like all my first friends he calls me Sammy. "Nowadays," he wrote, "the past seems near and the present far away—far away from so much of my life that matters. How is it with you, Sammy? What do you think?" I read the letter to Vicki. "Well, Sammy," she said, "what do you think?" "I don't know. Don't know," I said, laying the letter down gently on the kitchen table and suddenly feeling very sad. "I don't know."

1

The Road

I read Cormac McCarthy's *The Road* on a flight from Adelaide to Perth. In the seat next to me sat a woman traveling to the funeral of her father. That morning he died unexpectantly, and throughout the flight the woman burst into tears. "I'm so sorry," she said repeatedly. "There, there, my dear, don't worry about it," I said, marking my place in the book and patting her on the back. "Oh, my, I am making this trip hard for you," she said. "But I can't help it. I loved my father so much." "You are right to cry," I said. "What sort of person would you be if you didn't weep?" When the plane landed, I hadn't gotten far down the road. But that was all right. McCarthy's landscape was ashen and forbidding, and I decided to reverse direction and head back toward where I started eight decades ago. I knew sections of the road would be corrugated and potholed, and the shoulders, overgrown and weedy. I expected to see trash in the roughage of undergrowth. But that, too, was all right. Perhaps I'd spot a couple of Royal Crown Cola bottles. If the road wound through Nashville, I'd probably notice the wrappings of Goo Goo Clusters. On each package appeared a round, lumpy Goo Goo with a mouth-sized hunk bitten off. Made from chocolate, caramel, marshmallow nougat, and roasted peanuts, the candies were cavity-chiselers. They were too sweet for my taste, and like the person implied by the illustration on the wrapper, one bite would have been enough, no matter my hunger.

Still, if the road dribbled into Georgia, I could stop at B. Lloyd's and buy pecans. I might purchase fireworks, Roman candles and a few packages of pop crackers, as my boyhood friends and I called them. Seventy years ago, we had glorious fireworks battles, shouting and running, laughing, shooting candles, and tossing pop crackers. I wasn't sure what I'd do with my purchases from B. Lloyd's. A last grand fireworks fight would be fun, but that was impossible. My young opponents had mustered out of life. For the record, I never bought amputating ashcans or cherry bombs. My pop crackers were small and safe. More startling than loud, their explosions were just "the ticket," I recalled, to make a busy mother jump and shout "Jesus." If I met a repressed boy wearing a Little Lord Fauntleroy suit, I'd give him the firecrackers and tell him to surprise his mother. "Set them off beneath the dining room window when her bridge club sits down for lunch then run like Hell," I'd suggest. "How your mother will giggle!" Of course, well-dressed urchins now exist only in forgotten books, and I knew that the possibility of meeting a boy sporting a velvet suit with a lace collar was nonexistent. Probably, I'd tote the fireworks for a while and mull the past. Eventually they'd become a nuisance, and I'd submerge them in a pool beside the road. Once they became waterlogged, I'd shred them to prevent their starting fires.

I didn't decide where I'd dump the remnants—recycle or trash cans, storm drain, or simply scattered in wet ditches. On the road not only does one concern push another out of mind but roadways themselves often become unclear. They meander and fork, sometimes with purpose, other times aimlessly, hither and thither into hazes and sunshine, into fictions and almost-truths. In addition to childhood companions who exploded across summer days like brocades or crossettes, fireworks made me recall quieter old acquaintances, boys and girls who were sparklers, classmates who burned bright and shiny for a moment then disappeared. I spent a morning beside the road searching for them on the internet. Most of the boys had died or, flaring out, had drifted into anonymity. A few girls still flickered. My date at my college graduation in 1963 was prettier and smarter than me. At the end of the weekend, we said goodbye. I headed east to Britain, and she went west to California and a career that earned her a biography on the internet. The biography stated that she was born in 1951. "It is a wonder I wasn't arrested. If the dean realized my date was twelve years old, he might have withheld my degree," I told my friend Josh. "No, you naughty boy, nothing would have happened. You were in Tennessee. If the girl had been born in 1957, you might have gotten into a tad of difficulty. At the worst her first-grade teacher would have made you stand in the hall and spend recess inside."

"We'll kill the old red rooster when she comes" is out of date. Roosters still lose their heads but not to cooks preparing dishes of chicken and dumplings. Medical technicians now supervise beheadings. Instead of drumsticks, combs matter. They contain a lubricating jelly which is injected into aching knees to ease joint pain. What ligaments linger in my right knee are thinner than dental floss. As a result, I limp. To add hop to my step and help me continue along the road, a doctor gave me a shot of rooster-comb. I didn't crow, but before leaving the building, I addressed the receptionists saying, "look out hens." Once upon a time, in the way-back Yonder, my words might have caused clucking and scurrying. Now they provoked laughter, punctuated by the remark, "Oh, Mr. Pickering, you are such a bird."

On the road I negotiated my way over a few bumps. Most were small and resembled rumble strips more than gullies or frost heaves. All portions of my walk were calm. Indeed, for anxious readers who occasionally joined me, my meanderings must have been wondrously boring and thus more therapeutic than Alprazolam. As Time passes, walkers and paths change. Both become more mellow. Sharp inclines soften into pleasant ups and downs, and silent creek beds sing, more melodiously after a listener ages and his hearing becomes less acute. In hindsight one realizes that the dry stony plains that once forced him to lace his heart in a hard-heeled boot weren't as arid and rocky as he thought. Now I know that even when I thought myself an outcast, I wasn't one. I was always comfortable, preternaturally at home in the world, a state of being that siphoned air out of rancor and palliated fervor, creating satisfaction and peace of mind. Over the years it cooled my prose, making my becoming a grievance collector impossible on the page and off.

Shortly after I got the rooster shot and before I walked farther, the hot water heater in my house in Storrs ruptured and flooded the basement. A couple of days later Vicki and I spent a morning ripping a bale of ivy out of the only smoketree on campus. Ivy is a vigorous strangler, and so I crawled under the branches of the tree and clipped the ivy at its roots. In the past I rescued magnolias from vines. Every spring I imagine their blossoms to be thank-you notes. Sometimes I think pulling vines out of trees the most significant thing I've done at the university. As I ambled, I recited fragments of old poems. The poems were lyrical and soothing, sleepy with simple rhymes and rhythms. Typical were four lines by Mortimer Collins. "O whisper at eventide, wind of the west, / When the shadowy valleys are lying at rest, / When through the dim lanes as wayfarers pass, / They hear the long sweep of the scythes in the grass."

Collins lived in the nineteentg century, and although I sauntered, the road led me into a past far from McCarthy's present. Perhaps leaving a literary moment is possible only if a reader saunters. The by-ways of libraries and used bookstores are often deserted and forlorn. But if a walker pauses and explores the stacks, he'll unearth books iridescent with pleasures. On my desk is a copy of *Miss Toosey's Mission* by Evelyn Whitaker. First published in the 1870s, the book was a popular Sunday School prize. Printed in 1891 and bound in red cloth and beige boards, decorated with gold leaves on the front cover and gold lettering on the spine, my volume was likely a presentation copy. Although not presented to me, the book was a surprising, spirit-boosting gift. Evelyn Whitaker wrote some twenty-five books, two-thirds of them published before 1900 and all anonymous until the first years of the twentieth century. While perusing advertisements attached to L. T. Meade's novels for girls, I stumbled across *Miss Toosey.* On a whim I bought the book. Whim has long influenced my reading, as it does that of many amateur bibliophiles. Actually, it has affected the course of my life. How nice to be a rambler free from the barbed rigor of purpose and able to sail with or against changeable winds, not only Collins's west wind but those blowing from the east, south, and north.

Miss Toosey is warm and gentle, inspiriting, not a fine book, but a bettering book, one that brightens thought, and for a happy moment quickens appreciation of others and helps a reader forget the soiling irritants of social life. "Miss Toosey," the story began

> always wore a black silk dress on Sunday, and went three times to church. Morning, afternoon, and evening, as soon as the bell changed at the quarter, that black silk dress came out of Miss Toosey's little house in North street, turned the corner into High street, crossed the Market-place, passed under the archway into the churchyard, in at the west door, and up the middle aisle, past the free seats, which occupy the lower end of Martel church, and stopped at the second pew on the left-hand side.

In her hands she carried a prayer book, hymnal, spectacle case, an umbrella, and a little brown bible. Pressed between leaves of the bible was a bouquet of faded flowers. Miss Toosey was an angular spinster. Once when her face was round and smooth, she'd had a "simple girlish romance" and her heart overflowed with happiness. But the love ended, and for night after night afterward she fell asleep sobbing, her cheek pillowed on the brown bible. Now in old age she had little money. As a girl she had received no practical education and had learned only to make wax flowers, crochet, play tunes laboriously on a piano, and speak a few words of what was supposed to be French. She lived a small life in her little house, her only companions being Sammy the cat and Betty a maid.

Hers was a life practically unlived except for a quiet almost unmarked moment. One morning in church a young barrister noticed her listening to a sermon. The sermon wasn't eloquent, and, Whitaker wrote, Miss Toosey's face was "a common, little, wizen old-maidish face, with nothing intellectual or noble about it." Yet, she continued, it was "transfigured into something like beauty with the brightness of a reflected light." Such is the source of love. Whitaker then addressed readers who had lost the capacity to be affected by the everyday. "Don't you know," she asked, "how sometimes a scrap of broken glass on a dust heap will catch the sunlight and shine with quite dazzling brilliancy, and how a little smutty raindrop in a London court will hold the sun and a gleaming, changing rainbow in its little mirror?" It is a passage I'd read to students if I were still teaching. I wouldn't rage against indecency and injustice. I'd pose Whitaker's question.

Whitaker was a smart and appealingly sensible writer, a novelist, yes, but also a closet essayist with a nourishing vein of preacher in her character. Because small children were "not tall enough to see troubles," she opined, they were "cheerful souls" content "with life as seen from near the ground, which is, I fancy, a much more amusing point of view than we enjoy." Quite so—frequently to see far is both to see too much and to see too little. Whitaker avoided explaining the inexplicable, a temptation to writers crafting well-made tales. in fact, a temptation to all people in conversation or on the page, and, of course, a temptation more enduring than a recurrent fever to teachers. Whitaker never mentioned "whim." In recounting the visit of the young barrister to Miss Toosey, Whitaker said she didn't know what impelled him. "It is impossible to define motives accurately, even our own. We cannot say why we do a thing; every reason may be against it—common sense, habit, inclinations, experience, duty, all may be pulling the other way, and yet we tear ourselves loose, and do the thing urged by some invisible motive of whose existence we are hardly conscious."

Miss Toosey often slept through sermons, later explaining that she "closed her eyes to pay better attention." The Missionary Bishop to the African Diocese of Nawaub delivered the sermon that captured the attention of Miss Toosey and during which John Rossiter, the barrister, noticed her. At the service the Martel choir sang Reginald Heber's moving missionary hymn, "From Greenland's icy mountains, / From India's coral strand." Afterward Miss Toosey decided to go on a mission. When Rossiter came to her house, she was preparing herself by reading "an old book called 'Voyages and Adventures.'" It was open at a page depicting a "cannibal feast" in which a man was being roasted. Dancing around him were banqueteers sporting feathers, necklaces, and rings, but not wearing clothes. Not used "to fashionable picture-galleries where Eves and Venuses, in unadorned beauty, are admired and criticized by the sensible young people of the present day," Miss Toosey blushed at being discovered perusing such a book. Because they were cannibals, she explained to Rossiter, the natives didn't look quite so naked. "I always think," she said, "a white pig is more indecent-looking than a black one."

Did Miss Toosey go on a mission? No, of course, not, but she had an effect on Rossiter, and if the many printings of Whitaker's book indicate anything, she may have affected a goodly number of readers. Near the end of the story, Miss Toosey died. "There was nothing grand or striking in Miss Toosey's death," Whitaker wrote, "there very rarely is; it is only now and then that there is a sunset glory over this life's evening." The book affected me. I have left the road for a while though taking a break may have been caused more by my lawn mower's exploding than by the story of Miss Toosey. Whatever the reason I found a nice shady rest stop. Summer is here; days are hot, and I'll rest my knee and savor a little temporary oblivion, as Miss Toosey described one of her naps in church. Of course, I'll read. Because *Miss Toosey's Mission* delighted me, I purchased *Tip Cat*, another of Whitaker's books. For a handful of dollars, I bought the first American edition published in 1885. The novel is one of those rare books a reader likes so much that he studiously staggers through the pages, stopping continually to prevent reaching the conclusion. The tale so appeals to me that I may even hide it and pretend to lose it for a few days.

No book lover could race through a tale that begins:

> When there was a funeral at a house on the other side of the street, Latty and Sybil were allowed to stand at the nursery window, and watch all that went on, though nurse would not allow them to have the window open and to lean out, as she and Martha [a servant] did, to see it turn the corner into the square, but the children saw a great deal, and for weeks after, funerals was their favorite game, and they even persuaded nurse to dress the doll Sybil had received on her birthday as a widow.

The Scout motto "Be Prepared" originated in the underground stacks of a library, not in the rocky wilds of a fictional wasteland. I may not return to the road for a while. Yesterday I ordered an old copy of Whitaker's *Laddie* from a used-book dealer in Grand Rapids, Michigan. Published in 1879, *Laddie* was a popular Sunday School prize like *Miss Toosey*. "Oh, happy, happy Small Expectations!"

2

'Tis the Season

St. Nicholas doesn't hitch his reindeer to our chimney anymore. In December Vicki still makes tins of Viennese Crescents, Mincemeat Bars, Sugar, and Chocolate Walnut Refrigerator Cookies. She mails them to family, but no longer does she set a bale of them and a trough of milk out in the living room on Christmas Eve for Santa's four-legged guys and gals. Holidays are Telephone Days. On Thanksgiving Vicki prepared a festive lunch: turkey, sweet potatoes and apricots, and string beans. She made dressing and gravy, cranberry sauce, and an apple pie. Enjoying the meal were only four of us, Vicki and I, Francis and his friend Eddie. The rest of the family were landlines away. Francis said he'd arrive at 10:30. He appeared at three o'clock. "I decided to stain my deck," he said, handing Vicki a homemade quince pie as a peace offering. The pie was good, but it did not dispel the impression that duty not inclination brought Francis to the house. Lunch became dinner. We drank champagne, ate both pies, and had a nice time. Although the late meal wasn't flat, the evening didn't bubble, and I went to bed at 8:30.

At Christmas Vicki and I lifted a verb from Clement Moore and dashed away. For oldsters, real holidays are respites from the presences of family and friends and their concerns and worrisome conversations, nagging matters which a person can rarely alleviate. Vicki and I wished everyone Merry Christmas then decamped for three weeks, spending five days in Fort

Lauderdale and sixteen days cruising the Caribbean with thirteen hundred passengers on Holland America's *Zaandam*, one of the line's smaller ships. The trip was familiar. Vicki and I had cruised the Caribbean several times, but as a person ages, repetition doesn't simply become more appealing, it becomes seductive, offering the palliative comfort of the expected. However, eschewing the new or the spontaneous doesn't completely free the elderly from worry. If one's twenties and thirties are the decades of antic behavior, then the seventies and eighties are the decades of worry. Awareness of past experiences grinds through the mind like rocks in a tumbler. Twice while Vicki and I were on cruises, the car battery died. This December before leaving Storrs, I bought a new battery to ensure the motor would turn over when we fetched the car from the long-term parking lot at the Hartford airport. I also purchased new tires in case snow was falling while Vicki and I drove to the airport or the roads became icy in our absence—as they had done in the past. I didn't fret about catching the virus. Not only had Vicki and I had the virus, but afterward we'd received a broadside of preventive shots. Instead, I worried about suitcases, imagining ours going astray during the flight to Fort Lauderdale. I got in such a pother that I dreamed about bags. In one dream, red brick row houses stretched through and beyond the distance. Below the last step on the stoop in front of each house sat three large suitcases open and ready for me to pack. Of course, even on blue deckchair days a person cannot shed nagging concerns. "Do you think Mr. Mooney remembered to repair the chimney?" Vicki asked on Eagle Beach in Aruba. "I hope Harp Plumbing followed our instructions and installed a new sump pump in Barbara's house across the street," I answered, the mention of one worry resuscitating another.

The flight to Fort Lauderdale went well. But it was not without incident. Sitting in the row across from me were two men. The man beside the aisle was a dandy. He had a goatee, and his hair was coiffed and moussed. He wore a watch with more dials than a power plant and a waist-pinching neon blue sport coat. From the left upper pocket an orange handkerchief toppled out bright as a daylily. In the seat next to him sat a grizzled old man. The man brought the ingredients of lunch with him. After the flight got under way, he began making a sandwich, laying out slices of bread and atop the bottom piece placing ham, lettuce, and cuts of tomato. He then produced a plastic packet of mayonnaise. The packet was sealed, and as the man struggled to tear the top open, it exploded, pelting his neighbor. "What have you done?" the neighbor exclaimed. "Do you know what you have done?" "Sorry about that. Just like birdshot," the old man said, extracting a Kleenex from his trousers. "Let me wipe you off," he continued, leaning over. The scene smacked of Abbott and Costello. All that remained necessary was Abbott's whacking Costello on the side of the head. "No," the neighbor responded. "Don't touch me. My god, you have turned my coat into a salad." "Yes, and I'm sorry. But these damn packets always give me fits. I'm not the only person who has trouble with them, no siree," the old man said. "I bet you've had trouble, too. But I'll tell you what. How about eating half my sandwich? That should square us. It'll be tasty. The tomatoes and lettuce are from my garden, and I bought some nice meat on the way to the airport. It's smoked and has got a thick brown sugar glaze." "Sandwich! I don't want a sandwich," the man said. "This was a Brunello jacket."

Vicki and I no longer mail Christmas cards. Instead after Christmas I write notes to individuals who sent us cards.

Anticipating that traveling would tire me, I got the jump on my January duty, and early in December wrote people whom I expected to send me cards. I beat all my acquaintances to the post office except a nonagenarian living in my father's hometown Carthage, Tennessee. Every Christmas she sends a lengthy letter in which she describes the doings of families, the names of which Father would have recognized but which I do not know. Nevertheless, I always write a long reply. The world of a retired teacher is small, and I liked learning about the lives of strangers. Moreover, while I read, I recalled days spent in Carthage visiting Grandma and Grandpa Pickering. I laid my pen down and remembered rubbing Scarlet, Grandma's cat, until purring became a song. In Nashville I lived in an apartment, and I loved the mellow outdoor fragrance of Grandpa's small patch of burley. I liked searching for fat green hornworms on the tobacco after which I grazed Grandpa's rows of strawberries, eating so many that I became a juvenile St. Nicholas, turning my "little round belly" into a "bowlful of jelly." Time is a relentless diminisher. This year my correspondent did not send a letter. Instead, I received a small card on which she wrote three sentences. In the first she reported that she suffered from an arthritic knee and her husband from a bad disc in his neck. Then she concluded saying, "No news in Carthage! Sanderson Funeral Home continues to provide comfort to many."

Vicki and I live closeted lives. Cards like the one from the woman unlock the closet door. Shortly after receiving the card, I wrote instructions for the disposition of my carrion after I took the big jump: no funeral, no memorial, no obituary, and cremation in a cardboard mummy-case. "Don't store my ashes in the basement beside the washing machine. They'll molder, and you might mistake them for a fumigant. Dump them in the side yard while they are dry and fresh." "Old women are never obedient. Vicki will ignore your wishes," my friend Ben said. Ben spoke from familial experience. His grandfather owned a farm beside the Duck River in Tennessee. On his deathbed he told his wife that he wanted to be cremated and asked her to scatter his ashes above his favorite fishing hole. Instead, she dressed him in a pair of red and blue striped pajamas, slapped him into a mahogany half-couch casket, and buried him in the family plot. "This way, I can keep my eye on him," she told members of her canasta club. "I didn't let him stray when he was alive, and I'll be damned if he starts now because I can't drag him to attend church every Sunday."

What really opens the closet door is travel. In Fort Lauderdale we didn't behave differently than we did in Storrs. Instead of being startled by the occasional card, we roamed Las Olas and Seabreeze Boulevards and read clothes. Taking a cue from *Sayings of the Desert Fathers*, a fifth-century collection of remarks by monks, I compiled *Statements on the Street.* "Storrs isn't Egypt, and our house isn't a cave," I told Vicki. "But we are reclusive—mongrelized anchorites." On the street, numbers of people wore shirts with statements printed across the fronts, probably to forestall conversation while simultaneously appearing opinionated, such things as "Whoever Voted for Biden Owes Me Gas Money" and "DeSantis 2024. Make America Florida." Bumper-plate statements are easier on the brain than thought. "Born Free. Taxed to Death" read a vanity tag attached to a Cadillac, the car ironically redder than the Russian Flag. "Insanity is all right so long as it remains within a family, but ostentatious lunacy peeves me," I said to Vicki. "An ant could walk across a pebble in Pakistan, and you'd take exception," Vicki said last week. Vicki exaggerates, but in the flesh I am more assertive than on the page. I asked a man wearing a shirt announcing, "Do I Care?" what he cared for or didn't care about. He didn't answer.

"I think it's a product name. My niece gave it to me," said a woman in a bakery wearing a shirt with "Fearless" stamped on the front in capital letters. "I'm actually quite shy." Not everyone in the bakery was retiring. Stamped on the front of a shirt worn by a woman was "I Drink Coffee Then I Do Things." Cleaning must have shrunk the shirt because it was too tight for comfort, that of the woman and that of other customers in the bakery. "Don't dare ask her about the shirt," Vicki said, "she's dangerous." I obeyed and fixing my eyes on the counter ordered an almond croissant. The unsolicited isn't always well-received, and instead of addressing passers-by, closet counselors wore shirts emblazoned with advice. "Live Your Life Like You Feel It" advised a shirt worn by an anorexic jogger. "Happy Sunday" declared another shirt. The wearer had escaped the mundane calendar because she wore the shirt on a Wednesday.

On city streets I am livelier than in my study. At home most people with whom I talk are imaginary. Days are so monastic in Storrs that the week before Vicki and I flew to Florida, I interviewed myself. The interview was concise, but, in its way, memorable and evocative—well, maybe not to folks incapable of fanciful listening. "Mr. Pickering," I asked. "What do you think about football?" "I don't think about football," I answered. "All right, then, Mr. P.," I asked, "What do you think about sex?" "I don't think about sex." My interrogator was persistent. "Okay, Mr. P., what do you think about when you are not thinking about things?" "When I am not thinking about things," Mr. P. responded, "I don't think about not thinking about things."

In Fort Lauderdale I occasionally muttered. Who wouldn't mutter on seeing a roughneck in a Trump baseball cap and wearing a wife beater on the front of which appeared "Sturgis Motorcycle Rally 2022." The sounds I made, however, were sotto voce, although the keen of ear might have distinguished the word *Covid.* In any case, I didn't subject myself to the inquisitorial because away from Connecticut my attar changed, making me cordial and receptive. Strangers stopped and questioned me, one man asking where he could purchase athletic socks. Oddly I knew because that morning I bought three pairs. Before finding them at CVS, I'd explored several stores all of which sold sweatshirts, bathing suits, towels, flip flops, and sun hats, clothing for a lively beach life. "The only woolly socks we sell are these," a woman said, holding up a pair of purple socks decorated with white clouds of popcorn. "They come in many colors—red, orange, green—for that special night at the movie," she said, adding, "they go well with M & M's." Observing my entering the Riverside Hotel on Las Olas, a man rushed after me. "Are you a dentist?" he asked. "Aren't you the dentist who fixed my teeth thirty years ago in the army?" I was startled and replied slowly. "Look at this," the man said opening his mouth, "you did a wonderful job. My teeth are still in good shape." "I'm sorry. I'm not a dentist," I said belatedly. "That doesn't matter," the man said. "Somebody who looks like you is a grand dentist."

On the *Zaandam*, passengers were generally retired. Many had reached wheelchair and walker years and were close to having their wills executed. "My husband is so lethargic," a woman said, "that I don't know if he is alive unless I shake him."

Bringing Christmas with them, passengers traveled with families, married sons and daughters and pre-school children. As could be expected, statements on shirts were sappy, a melody of "My Grandchild Loves Me" with variations, "My Favorite People Are My Grandchildren" and "I Adore My Little Annie." On the streets of Fort Lauderdale, rain forests of tattoos flourished, lianas and body parts blurring and turning blue in the sunlight. On the ship I noticed a single tattoo. On the right calf of a lumbering man was a Queen Anne armchair with cabriole legs, pad feet, and a back shaped like a vase. I'd never seen a tattoo of a chair, and I wondered if the man sported an attic of old furniture, a courting chair on a thigh or a loveseat on his back. Standing beside a hot tub, he wore a bathing suit and was shirtless. Surreptitiously, I circled him looking for other furnishings. The chair was his only tattoo. I speculated about its provenance. Did the man sell used furniture? Was he an amateur restorer? To escape a domestic harridan did he spend days in a woodshop imagining subjecting her to improvement by table saw? Maybe the chair belonged to a beloved grandmother, the woman who raised him after his mother died and his father became an alcoholic. Or maybe he was just a screwball. To my regret I did not immediately inquire about the tattoo.

Later, when near the pool or on a deck on which people were sunbathing, I studied calves, searching for other chairs. I didn't see any, probably because I was too occupied to be thorough. The *Zaandam* made twelve stops, eight in a row, none of which Vicki and I missed. Moreover, we don't participate in the bustle of cruise life. We have spent more than a year of our lives on cruise ships, but not once have we sunbathed, swum in a pool, gambled, or danced. We eat by ourselves, and at the conclusions of cruises we don't leave the ship with a pocket of calling cards given to us by acquaintances. Only once did I address one of the ship's officers, and that was to ask how many corpses could be stored in the morgue. "Three," the man replied, "but if it becomes necessary, we can stack them."

Thirty years ago, when I lectured on ships, we were social. But we have aged, and the effort spent building conversations with strangers often causes indigestion. Time rings multiple changes. No longer do I use a treadmill, broil in a sauna, or jog kilometers around the top deck. On land, guides call me Poppa. I don't climb small mountains, wander rocky nature trails, rappel down cliffs, or bucket through rapids. When I swim in the ocean slight waves knock my legs about like seaweed making hauling myself out of the water impossible without Vicki's help. One morning as I walked through the Lido breakfast room carrying a cup of tea, two middle-aged women hurried over to me. "Stop," they commanded, "one of your shoes is untied. We have to fix it, or you'll fall." They ignored my assertion that I could tie the shoe. "No," they said firmly, "you might topple and hurt yourself." Before I could protest, one woman was kneeling on the floor tying my shoe while the other steadied me, holding my free arm. "Gee," I said to Vicki later. "That was nice, but am I really that feeble?" Silence is often more accurate than words. Vicki did not answer.

I did not take binoculars or field guides on the cruise. On past trips I packed a natural history library. Like me the natural world has aged during the immediate past. It has emptied and become less robust. The flocks of boobies that used to accompany cruise ships whirling and diving for flying fish are gone. No longer do squadrons of great frigate birds ride thermals over the harbor of St. John's in Antigua. Saint Martin's sugar birds or bananaquits don't swarm gaily almost laughing, and few colonies of cattle egrets cling to shoreline scrub looking like handkerchiefs. Perhaps worse, at least personally, two days before leaving Connecticut I found Effie my red-tailed hawk dead on the shoulder of Storrs Road. A car had crushed her into patties of gristle and feather. For years Effie perched on a limb outside my study. She recognized me and I, her. I knew where she nested, and I watched her raise her fledglings. In the spring when Vicki and I had tea in the driveway, Effie often flew into a nearby red maple, just, it seemed, to be near us.

Aged cruisers don't like radical change. They value repetition. It lessens anxiety and buttresses the unspoken hope that they and their worlds are stable. Vicki and I travel not to see anew but to awaken memory and, if possible, relive happy experiences. Discovering that the Waterfront Café on the Careenage in Bridgetown, Barbados, had closed disheartened us. Every time we were in Barbados, we had lunch there, sitting at water's edge, drinking Banks beers and eating flying fish sandwiches. On this trip we ate elsewhere. The restaurant was pleasant, but the meal didn't nudge dozing memories into thoughts. Although familiar paths frequently lead to disappointment, rarely do they end in tedium. Invariably I notice something overlooked in the past. In Holetown I read memorials attached to the walls of St. James Parish Church. How on previous trips to Barbados had I missed the marble tablet "Sacred to the Memory of Dames Christine and Jane Abel successively the Consorts of Sir John-Gay Alleyne, Baronet"?

Born in Barbados in 1724 and dying there in 1801, Alleyne was a member of the House of Assembly for forty years and on several occasions served as speaker. The memorial resembled a classical scroll and unraveled in a series of elegant irregular lines. Alleyne's wives were "Women in whose praise

Encomium has to borrow no false Colouring from Flattery and of whom no Language can describe the Loss!" Alleyne lived thirty-one years of "unspeakable Felicity" with his first wife. With his second, he lived "little more than fourteen...In that short Period She bless'd him with the Birth of seven lovely Infants, the eldest of which John-Gay-Newton Alleyne, a Boy of Hopes commensurate to the fondest Wishes of a Father, in thirteen Summers was too ripe for Immortality for longer Continuance upon Earth."

In 1745 Thomas Warton wrote "The Pleasures of Melancholy," in which he celebrated among other things, "tapers dim," "twilight cells and bowers," "the screech-owl's note," and "the lowly cricket's drowsy dirge"—delights "which alone the pensive soul can taste." To me the memorial scroll was a lachrymose marvel of decorous prose, not congenial to the guffawing present that urges people to smile so that the world smiles with them. The scroll was a melancholy elegy dampening the cheeks while softening the heart. It appealed to people who'd weathered into being unable to escape awareness of the "fleeting state of things." To others in the "purple Spring" of their sportive lives it was probably disconcerting if not boring. "The afflicting Intelligence" of the death of John-Gay-Newton Alleyne at Eton "arrived but one day late enough to spare his expiring Mother such Pangs as she was incapable of feeling for her own Dissolution but such as the Mournful Erecter of this three fold Monument of the Instability of all human Enjoyments for the sake of his surviving Children and in silent Resignation to the Wisdom that ordains it must labour to endure." "Vicki," I said. "You must read this." "No," she said, "if you are that enthusiastic, it has to be sad."

How different was our mood and how Vicki and I enjoyed sitting once again outside Barbie's in Cockburn Town on Grand Turk, eating a double order of conch fritters and drinking Turk's Head beer. How nice to revisit Café Sombras in San Juan and treat ourselves to brandy cake and drink cappuccinos, the cream atop the coffee swept into gentle hearts. We smiled on seeing a familiar crowd milling around the steps of the Cathedral of San Felipe Apostol: a man hawking corn to attract pigeons; bead, wooden box, and straw hat sellers, then a tout cajoling tourists into being photographed with two blue and yellow hyacinth macaws. On previous cruises Vicki and I wandered the grounds of the Cathedral of St. John's in Antiqua. We read headstones and picked up trash. Then the cathedral was closed having been wrecked by the big and the little, storms and termites. During the pandemic the interior had been rebuilt with cedar and pine. "I haven't been here in three years," I said to the docent at the door. "Welcome home," he replied, smiling and the bougainvillea on the grounds suddenly seemed to burst into blue and red celebrations. Unlike the young whose lives jitter too rapidly for them to indulge in sentimentality, the old have the leisure and inclination to appreciate the maudlin.

Eight years ago, in the Castries Central Market in St. Lucia, I purchased a wooden lion carved from West Indian mahogany by a Rastafarian vendor. The lion was nine inches long and five high. It was too light for our bathroom scales, and Vicki estimated that it weighed as much as a pound of butter, with a nip sliced off one end. When people buy objects the appearances of which are more grotesque than representational, they sometimes explain their tastes by calling their purchases folk art. The carving appealed to me because it was and wasn't a lion, a bit like my imagined life, conventional but also slightly off kilter and idiosyncratic. During the cruise I revisited the vendor. I remembered him, and he remembered me. I knew that he took care of his mother and uncle. He knew I lived in Connecticut and had bought a lion. He had carved another lion, this one bigger, eleven inches long, six and a half high, and weighing at least a pound and a half of butter, "closer to two pounds than to one," Vicki said. The animal's face looked more like that of a bulldog than that of a cat. Its tail curved over its back ending in a whisk broom, the bristles resembling bony human fingers, not tufted tassels. In the past I collected things to mark my passing, objects that would enrich quiet hours by reminding me I'd lived. That time had passed. I realized that my keepsakes would eventually be dispersed in a tag sale or vanish into a skip. As a result, nowadays I rarely buy anything. However, I bought the lion and didn't haggle over the price. To the vendor a few dollars mattered. To me they meant nothing. The lion now sits on a shelf in my study in front of volumes of my essays. Sometimes I take it and its predecessor down and rub their backs. "My pride," I tell Vicki.

For her part Vicki gathered inexpensive tokens to send to our children. Once home she packed the "treats" into boxes and mailed them. In a way the items were fragmentary records of our stops: from the Straw Market in Nassau small wooden dolphins and sharks, from Grand Bahamas actual straw animals, two dogs, both mongrels, one tall, the other short, and from the market in Castries colorful patterned baskets, right for clementines and apples on a kitchen table. For refrigerator doors she bought fish magnets in Antigua, their surfaces foil under acrylic and glimmering like scales. In Barbados at the "Art Glass" shop, she purchased hanging knick-knacks,

Christmas trees, fish, and a blue turtle. From a stall on the dock at Fort-de-France in Martinique she bought small, beaded hummingbirds with dangling gold and silver tail feathers, and on Santa Domingo earrings shaped like hearts, one ventricle amber, the other light blue larimar. Among other treats, Vicki bought chocolate, coffee, and hot sauces. The articles she collected were trinkets, but to me seemed weightier than the expensive hoardings, and doings, of the mighty and powerful, the colorful and famous, "the regrettable people," as they are known. Age clears one's vision and levels. Unless a person suffers from socially induced glaucoma, he eventually abjures hierarchies and becomes an apostate to branding ambition, elevated tastes, and high seriousness.

In *I Have Been Assigned the Single Bird*, Susan Cerulean calls the natural world "our true home and our church." I am not churched. But home is where a person recognizes plants and animals. Despite being far from Connecticut I wasn't away from home. The Caribbean islands were gardens of the familiar: mottled poisonwood, bauhinia butterflied with orchids, the salver-like leaves of blue mahoe, bushes of sea grape and wild lettuce, and poinciana with black wrinkled ferules. Casuarina reminded me of Western Australia. Aristocratic royal palms towered above bourgeois silver palms. Yellow bells were music to the eye, and breadfruit gleamed, its leaves greased and slicked for a night on the town, while coral vine wound across hillsides and through scrub like dental floss. A blue-crowned motmot glowed amid the knots of a rainforest, and a troupial flew into a divi-divi, its black hood becoming a bib slipping down over its orange breast. Many trees leaped from memory: on Saint Martin the great kapok beside the house of Ruby Bute, an artist, and in Castries the old raintree in Derek

Walcott Square. Next to the porch at Barbie's on Grand Turk, Cordia welcomed us with bouquets of red blossoms. In a vacant lot Caribbean milkweed was pink and purple with small flowers. Above Ocho Rios, African tulip trees smoldered like embers across the lush hillsides of Saint Ann. The list of plants was almost endless, but not to recognize and appreciate numbers of them was not to live, not to realize that the world is, can be, and should be a paradise.

Only when root rot invades his bark and sours his heartwood does an oldster lose the hankering for foolishness. In mathematical terms, old age is the time of subtraction, a realization that irks me. Accordingly at the *Zaandam*'s last stop at Freeport in Grand Bahama, I signed Vicki and me up for a twelve-and-a-half-mile bicycle ride. Vicki and I prepped for the ride by walking the Lind Point Trail on St. John, 1.14 miles running from the island's Visitor Center to Honeymoon Beach. The trail meandered through cactus scrub festooned with morning glories and pink butterfly vines. Five years ago, I'd have waltzed the path. But both the trail and I had eroded. The ground was rocky and slippery. Moreover, I was tottery, and my waltz occasionally deteriorated into a jitterbug, punctuated by the exclamation, "Oh, shit!" Still, I didn't fall. The only surprise came after I picked a stick off the ground to steady myself and a swarm of termites surged across my hand, and treating my arm as a bridge, clamored atop my shoulder then bustled itching down my back. At the beach an Island Sammy beer proved a powerful insecticide, and the termites disappeared.

When participants for the bicycle ride gathered on the dock, the guide called me Grandpoppa, and Vicki observed that I was forty years older than all the other riders except her.

While Vicki rode a conventional bicycle with hand breaks and several speeds, I rode a coaster brake bike with a low-slung oversized seat and swept-back handlebars that looked like antlers. After six miles my legs were buttery. After a dozen, they became margarine. I lagged, but nevertheless I didn't fall behind. Vicki was last because she wanted to be available to shovel me up if I experienced a punctured heart. I urged her to peddle ahead, but she didn't obey. The landscape was flat, and the ride wasn't insect-ridden, strenuous or particularly interesting. For the most part we rode across barrens, portions of which had been scraped into housing developments, other sections of which were failed developments. Yellow pines thrived in the scrub looking tall and leggy, "wild runway models," Vicki said. At the conclusion of the ride, I was wobbly but in good spirits. I had not climbed a mountain or zip-lined across a canyon, but I was eager for another small, cardio-vascular test.

Reading people travel with books. The only book I brought onto the *Zaandam* was Turgenev's *A Sportsman's Notebook*, a luminous collection of short stories describing rural life in mid-nineteenth-century Russia. Cruises are lowbrow. Shipboard distractions don't elicit thought. As a result, travelers have the mental leisure to read memorable books, the reading of which elsewhere might exhaust them. The *Notebook* was the only "great" volume I read. Unlike newer ships the *Zaandam* had a library. Most of the volumes were well-traveled, broken-spined, and had been the library on another Holland America ship, probably the *Prinsendam*, since sold out of the fleet. Among the books I read were Jack London's *Sea Wolf*, Alan Furst's thriller *Mission to Paris*, and Hunter S. Thompson's *The Rum Diary*, a bibulous record begun in 1959 when Thompson was twenty-two and working and writing in San Juan. I read a shelf of other books, but all were like shoes picked up at the Salvation Army. I tried them on, wore them for a while, then returned them to the library, thumbed but unremembered.

A single book cannot determine life unless a reader is so sectarian he ignores what is actually written and sees only what enforces his convictions. However, a book can influence a moment or maybe two. Before leaving Storrs, I read George Singleton's *Staff Picks*, a volume of Singleton's rakingly bright and funny stories. In one tale, Renfro Truluck speculates about the effects of Columbus's finding "us." If Columbus had landed on another continent, Renfro points out, the Indians would not have been slaughtered and there would have been no Civil War, no Depression, and no Vietnam. "A brilliant conversational prophylactic," I thought, and when strangers unexpectedly addressed me on the ship, immediately I asked if they ever considered what their lives would have been had the trade winds become confused and blown Columbus away from the new world. I kept Singleton's reference to the Civil War. But I tarted up my statement a little. "Think about it," I said, "there would have been no Civil War, no Coca Cola, no Social Security, no state of Alabama, no labradoodles, no Democrats, no Jimmy Dickens telling folks to take a cold tater and wait, and no goddamn Super Bowl with sex fiends twerking at halftime." Of course, I varied the menu of things cited, particularly the foodstuffs. Occasionally, I mentioned grandma's dog hair-laced tomato aspic, Heinz's 57 varieties, and Sweet Baby Ray's barbeque sauce. Twice I stirred in Dijon mustard but removed it from the ingredients when auditors looked puzzled. Once when a listener looked sane, I substituted Republicans for Democrats. But if the truth must be told, no matter the items I cited reactions to my conversation starter were the similar.

Words misfired. Eyes blinked, and heads waggled as if the creeping palsy had taken "holt." A couple of people broke well but stumbled at the barrier of "uh." No one who addressed me approached again. On noticing me ahead of her in a hallway a woman reversed direction and hurried away as if she'd remembered an item in her cabin. "What do suppose that woman thinks about you?" Vicki said. "I don't know," I said. "Thinking is for the young. Living is hard enough for the old."

After disembarking, Vicki and I stayed three days in Fort Lauderdale, "The False Eyelash City," as a journalist dubbed it. Mischiefs of female inhabitants wear long black false eyelashes. The lashes curl up sharp, inflexible, and steel hard. If attached to plough trucks, they could scrape ice off highways and never wear out. At an art fair on Las Olas, Vicki bought "Midnight Gazer" a six-inch square oil painting on wood by a man who dubbed himself "Artist & Practicing Troublemaker." All the colors were shades of blue and gray. In the painting, a dumpy man lay on his back atop a snail shell, facing up and gazing through the night at the stars. Poking out of the shell was a hedgehog. The painting was a whimsical conversation piece, ideal for a small child's bedroom or, to be honest, an old man's study.

Initially after Vicki and I returned to Connecticut, the cruise seemed forgettable. But as cold settled around us, our experiences in the Caribbean grew beguiling. In our absence, nothing noteworthy occurred in Storrs. A member of the board of education sponsored a resolution urging students not to raise their hands in class. He called it a safety-measure. He said if President Biden noticed their hands in the air he'd shoot them down, asserting they were Chinese spy balloons. A phrenologist debated a forensic astrologer in a unitarian meeting hall;

various basketball teams won and lost games, and in a nearby town, the manager of a Walmart tried to control shopping cart traffic inside his store. After covid restrictions were lifted, Walmart customers started pushing carts recklessly, speeding, and causing T-bone and head-on collisions.

On side aisles, the manager posted "Slow Down" warnings depicting two carts colliding, their front wheels off the ground, the carts themselves ribby, looking like underfed male mountain goats in rutting season. At intersections where side aisles entered major thoroughfares, he erected blue and yellow Stop signs. All these signs faced the aisles. Atop each was a small whistle. It sounded like the siren on a state trooper's car and was triggered by a scoff-shopper's running the stop sign. Some of the most careless patrons were motorized shoppers, usually old people. "Reliving their salad days of peanuts and cotton candy at the state fair while driving bumper cars," the manager surmised. Curtailing the hot carters was easy. The manager installed governors on the store's battery-propelled carts. After learning about the manager's efforts to control aisle scoff-laws, my friend Josh emended Roy Acuff's "Wreck on the Highway," crooning "I heard the crash in the Walmart. There was cold cream and nail polish all together, but I didn't hear nobody pray, querido hermano. I didn't hear nobody pray, dorogoy brat."

Four days ago, Edward wrote from South Carolina and thanked Vicki for the "care package" of souvenirs. He reported that earlier in the week he took Sammy, our two-year-old grandson, to the zoo. "The juvenile orangutan was wandering about with a bucket on his head," Edward wrote. "Sammy does that at home." How dear, and funny, are the scenes of childhood, I thought, emending the first line of Samuel

Woolworth's "The Old Oaken Bucket." Despite Edward's sunny letter, the wind is in the East. The sky is dark and laden with snow and sailing away is once more in the offing. The afternoon after hearing from Edward, I walked downtown. On the way I spotted Lucy my skunk in the middle of Route 275. A car had flattened her. Lucy was almost entirely white, and one night two years ago I watched her dig yellow jackets out of the backyard. Because Lucy was a gentling part of my life, I hurried home, fetched a shovel, and pried her off the asphalt. I toted her some distance into a wood. She slipped off the shovel repeatedly, so eventually I seized her tail and carried her by hand. The ground was frozen, and I buried her beneath pancakes of dirt that I pried off the surface. On returning home, I put the shovel in the garage, washed my hands in the kitchen, and then going into the "back room" turned on the television. Somebody was playing football, and crowds were howling.

Lucy's death depressed me, and in hopes of raising my spirits, that evening I bought an after-Christmas present. Aside from used books so forgotten they cost less than ten dollars a volume, I hadn't purchased a material gift solely for myself in decades. From Ryder & Amies in Britain, I ordered a St. Catharine's College scarf, wool and claret with two pink stripes running parallel along its length. I once owned such a scarf, but like my years at Cambridge, it had been lost. Ordering the new scarf made me smile. The insignificant fury faded from the television, and as if I'd opened a scrapbook filled with old photographs, I saw a young me peddling down King's Parade headed for the boathouse. Ahead of me life shined like the sunrise. Wrapped around my neck and blowing over my back like celebratory bunting was my college scarf.

The next morning I received an unexpected email. "I BILL GATES," the email began, "decided to donate the sum of $5,000,000.00 USD to you as part of our charity project to improve 10 lucky individuals all over the world from our $65 Billion." Billy had done his homework, explaining that he'd prayed and searched the internet for people worthy his largesse. He selected me on seeing my "profile on Microsoft email owners list." Billy added that he was not getting younger, and not having "much time to live" wanted to help deserving individuals. "To facilitate the payment process," he requested that I send him my full name, residential address, occupation, age, telephone number, and home country. He neglected to ask for my Social Security and bank account numbers, oversights I knew he'd rectify in a later email. He concluded writing, "Remain Blessed Regards Mr. Bill Gates." Before I could follow Billy's instructions, the telephone rang. My pestiferous acquaintance Spam Risk had learned that my Caribbean cruise was over and that my credit card was again on dry land.

I was an old-school, square-rigged teacher, and nowadays at the university I sometimes feel "at sea." This morning Vicki and I walked our dogs on campus. As we sat on a bench sipping coffee, a girl asked if she could pet the dogs. She was a second-semester junior and a bright double major in engineering and ecology. We chatted, and I mentioned a handful of good teachers. Before leaving us and going to class, she said, "For once I talked to a tenured professor at UCONN." As Vicki and I started to leave, a second student asked to pet the dogs. She was an education major, and I asked if her male teachers wore coats and ties. "I don't have any male teachers," she said. Tonight, while cooking chicken, Vicki said, "You made that up about Walmart—didn't you?" "Certainly not," I answered. "But did you know several critics have called me a genius?" "Now, that really is a whopper," Vicki said, pouring herself a belt of cabernet sauvignon. "No, it's true. Obviously, you are oblivious to your husband's stature," I said, heading for the television and another evening of "Midsomer Murders." At the doorway I paused and said, "G-E-N-I-U-S is now leaving the kitchen." "What an odd way to spell horse's ass," Vicki replied then laughed, the timbre, if I may say so, inelegantly rough, a kind of hoarse cackling, more boiler than broiler, more drumstick than bosom.

3

Song

Songs frequently become imprinted on memory. As years pass, the words remain the same, but meanings change. Not long ago I listened to Gale Garnett's "We'll Sing in the Sunshine." I hadn't heard the song in six decades. Then, I thought it celebrated transient happiness and youthful effervescent passion. I imagined throwing my arm over a friend's shoulder. We'd smile, sing in the sunshine, and "laugh every day." I knew that eventually I'd "be on my way," not because my friend was unlovable but because "lavish" fantasies of pathless woods and lonely shores seduced me, "those ever-blooming sweets," as Mark Akenside expressed it, that charm the "inliven'd soul." I wasn't ambitious. I did not scorn place or custom. I was responsible, but I dreamed, as Byron put it, of what I could "ne'er express," I have aged into knowing both myself and the song better. Now it seems an anthem of reminiscence beyond the understanding of youth and appealing to the elderly evoking glimpses of lost friends and lost loves, indeed of a person's own lost selves, those beings who went their ways until the sun dimmed and the laughing quieted.

"We'll Sing in the Sunshine" was the first track on a dusty LP. In the second, Scott McKenzie urged travelers to San Francisco to wear flowers in their hair. I've never visited San Francisco. But before a crack in my memory bumped the needle out of the groove, I remembered hippies and their loose rainbow dresses, girls sweeter than jam: strawberry and raspberry, peach and rose petal. "Darn," I muttered, and the needle jumped. When I was young Tennyson's "Ulysses" was one of my favorite poems. What imaginative boy doesn't imagine drinking "life to the lees"? After a tedious classroom day, who doesn't ache for a real recess, roaming the "untravell'd world"? What youth envisions senescence and rusting unburnished, "as tho' to breathe were life," as the elderly Ulysses says? "Come, my friends," the tottery King exhorts his gray comrades urging them to leave Ithaca,

> 'Tis not too late to seek a newer world. / Push off, and sitting well in order smite / The sounding furrows; for my purpose holds / To sail beyond the sunset, and the baths / Of all the western stars, until I die.

Even in the aching Now when the waxen speech of Fox and CNN deadens my hearing, Ulysses' words cause my emotions to hiccup. But, of course, Ulysses' shipmates were too old to breast the roiling waves. They shouldn't have succumbed to the urgency behind the King's rhetoric. But after they sailed, they were so feeble they soon caught crabs causing their boat to be swamped before it passed the breakwater at the end of the harbor. Although Tennyson didn't record the aftermath of the boat's sinking, I know that Telemachus pulled his father from the sea. Unfortunately, water had filled the King's lungs, and despite efforts of the local Hippocrates, the King came down with "the old man's friend," pneumonia, and died at the foot of one of Ithaca's barren crags, far from the golden moonlit shores of the Happy Isles.

"And when our year has ended / And I have gone away," Garnett sang. "You'll say / We sang in the sunshine." Because she was young, Garnett was only partly correct. Long after that year and others, the middle-aged prune scrapbooks, shred letters, and cease humming except in the shower. They confine fantasy to the acceptable, and for a while hope the detritus of daily life will inhibit reminiscence. What oldster can bear receiving a letter from or writing a letter to one of the gentle people saying, "our baby would have been fifty this month"? Nineteen years ago, an old friend wrote me from England. In the letter he mentioned our literary careers. "Mine," he wrote describing his experience, "has been a little too stormy and wanton, but at 85 I still can work—a little lazily and without daring very much, but enough to fill a few hours a day." Paths through the final years of life are well-worn. Perhaps the elderly cannot do other than what people before them did. At 82 I still work, to be sure lazily and temperately, but enough to fill gaping hours and to minimize the undermining scour of reminiscence and its morose occasional consort regret.

Of course, a person cannot avoid reminiscences until after friends and acquaintances die. And in truth grieving is frequently gay. Deaths breathe life into comatose recollections. Rather than mourn, survivors often recall sunshine and laughter, days when the grass was greener and the sky bluer, indeed evenings haloed with embraces. Moreover, memory creates fictions, many of which please and invigorate. Years ago, did my classmate Freddy exercise himself into dehydration after which he raced to a dinner party? There, the story goes, he treated his thirst with a bottle of rosé causing him to collapse on the way home and convincing his wife he'd suffered a stroke. An ambulance carted him to a hospital where specialists subjected him and his insurance company to two days of tests, all of which revealed that he was parched but otherwise okay. When he visited his family doctor for a follow-up the next week, the doctor reassured him then said, "Freddy, there is a medical term for patients who behave like you." Did Freddy ask what the term was, and did the doctor say, "Asshole"? Oh, yes, and accounts of Freddy's irresponsible doings caused his close male friends to chuckle at his memorial service, pat one another on the back, and say things like "I hate to see good guys go up in smoke." As they left the church, instead of mouthing "Abide with Me" they almost shattered the death march of propriety and sang choice verses of "We're Off to See the Wild West Show."

When I am away from my desk, several things fill the hours, television not being one. A visual diet of sport, carnivals, gambling, murder, and news channels will give a rational person the jumps. It will also transform him into an anarchist or, if not that, a stoner addicted to injections of hair restorer and stool softener hopped up with liver pills, or so an escapee from a Southern Baptist male harem testified, this last according to an "in-the-know" social scientist. Retirement can be barren. Freedom frequently sucks the air out of days. Eventually many people miss the cage of schedule and bemoan the absence of work. Instead of being a dark metaphor for unending and unrewarding labor, the life of Sisyphus becomes alluring. Waking in the morning to small duties is better than waking to the lost feeling of having nothing to do. Once mowing the grass took three hours. Now because I have milk legs that throb after a few steps, mowing takes three days, one for the back yard, another for the front, the last for the sides. The peonies I planted twenty years ago no longer bloom, so last week I dug their roots and planted them under the clothesline in the back yard. None of the transplants will produce flowers, but the work filled two mornings. I occupied parts of eight other days shifting a rock exposed when the rotten woodpile behind the garage collapsed and tumbled backwards. The rock was oval and not thick, measuring twenty-six inches long, fifteen wide, and three and a half deep. Forty years ago, I'd have hoisted the rock and heaved it into the brush behind the house. This year I moved it by sliding my hands under one side and flipping it over. Each day I mustered the strength for four flips. Are such small doings gratifying? Not particularly, but they are occupying.

I also walk through hours, on Saturday and Sunday in woods along the Fenton River and on weekdays across the university campus. Vicki and the dogs accompany me. Mee walks beside us. But Jack is sixteen and tires quickly, so on the campus Vicki and I take turns rolling him in a small baby carriage. On weekdays we sit on a bench in the shade outside the art museum and sip coffee and share a chocolate croissant. We are fixtures like the realistic sculptures of people doing everyday things such as reading books or newspapers that one encounters in parks or on street corners in upscale neighborhoods. Passersby are generally in unnecessary hurries. They nod to us and smile at the dogs, but rarely do they pause. The paths we follow are familiar, and because my legs are weak, the walks are shorter and slower than the ambles of my middle years. After we finish our coffee, Vicki often leaves and pushes ahead with the dogs to get more exercise. I don't regret the slowness and the brevity of the walks. I pause often and talk to trees and flowers. Throughout the year but especially during the fresh months of a new year, retirees are gray absences, almost unnoticeable on the periphery of active doings. Because spring has arrived and plants are busy blooming and blossoming, they don't talk to me. I am an autumnal presence, out of season and negligible. Awareness of that doesn't bother me. Compliments result from observation and appreciation and do more for the feelings of people paying them than those receiving them. Telling the trees and flowers how much I admire their beauty makes me happy.

Behind the administration building I recently sat on a rock and studied old-fashioned blue Iris. They seemed eyes to the past. Time became hazy, and instead of sitting, I wandered Grandmother Pickering's country garden smelling her Iris. Flowers spilling from bridal wreath brought to mind hedges lining walks in the lost neighborhoods of imagination. To be sure the ornate can be moody, but it was just as appealing, the crimson cassocks covering English Hawthorns, and the sconces of pink and yellow panicles jumbled over horse chestnuts like the clutter decorating halls in affluent-turn-of-the century New York homes. In the shade the new leaves of copper beech gleamed like purple mats splashed with coffee. Redbud burst magenta and so mesmerizingly electric that a nearby wall vanished. Sunlight buffed the flowers on a tulip tree turning them into orange chalices—cups for communion with the grace of dirt. Panicles of flowers hung bunched on yellowwood like valences of thick white curtains. A fringe tree shook and swayed in the breeze and looked like the incarnation of the Holy Ghost. I always pause beside dogwood and rhododendron and on farm lanes under black cherry. Of course, the stops on my walks vary as flowers come and go and new leaves age. In the back yard as the fragrance of lilacs ebbs, ambrosial perfume rises from oriental bittersweet, at first mysterious because the flowers are tiny. Along the riverbank the trumpets of pink azalea or pinxter flower break my slow pace and force me to notice the buds on nearby mountain laurel. Last year's blooming was powdery. This year buds are thick, and flowers should blanket the bushes turning them into blizzardy mounds. In damp mosquito woods, thickets are white and cloudy with arrowwood, the fragrance gray and stuffy up close but on a distant breeze reserved and enticing.

Not only does walking fill hours but it forestalls unravelling, satisfies, and helps keep me in the study, not at my desk writing but in a chair reading, the chapters spelled by occasional naps on Grandfather Ratcliffe's old daybed. Age has changed my reading. I don't read for scholarly purpose, indeed for any clear purpose. I don't read to learn about life. Living has taught me plenty, "too damn much," I often think. Most of the books I now read are well over a hundred and twenty years old. I refuse to read contemporary reprints although most volumes I buy haven't been reprinted, at least not for a century. I purchase novels from used book dealers. None cost more than ten dollars including shipping. As a retiree I rarely get mail. Receiving the volumes is a treat and ordering them has made me eager to spot the mail truck turn onto Hillside Circle early in the afternoon. Worse for wear often means better for me, particularly if the wear includes inscriptions and notes, book plates, personal things that bring long-dead strangers to imaginary life.

How old was June Spaman when she read L. T. Meade's *Polly: A New-Fashioned Girl* in 1900? Did her siblings nickname her Firefly as the Maybright children did their sister Lucy, and did her aunt own an ankle-biting toy terrier named Scorpion? Did her older brother Bumpy put a toad under her pillow one night and did she call Baby Phil a "deader" at his funeral? As "First Prize" for "Regular Attendance" at the Linwood Church Sabbath School during the year 1914-15, a copy of Meade's *Outcast Robin* was awarded to Master James Murdoch. What kind of life did the sanctimonious little boy live after Master became Mr.? Before turning into a conventional spiritless adult, was he less saintly, and did he copy Hennery, Peck's Bad Boy, and one Sunday turn a basket of rats loose in church? Did he travel to Rome with his Pa and lure the Old Man into the catacombs by telling him they were going to a "leg show"? Did he light a roman candle then a giant firecracker inside one of the pyramids knocking bats and birds of ill omen "gally west" and terrifying tourists and their Arab guides, the latter crawling out into the sunlight on their hands and knees begging "Mr. Allah" to save them?

Recently I've read several books by Elizabeth Thomasina Meade Smith, on the title pages of her volumes appearing as L. T. Meade or Mrs. L. T. Meade. Born in 1844 and dying in 1914, Mrs. Meade wrote three hundred books. Genre didn't fence her, and she ranged the open country of writing, turning out, among others, historical and sentimental novels, religious stories, sensational tales, mysteries, and children's books. Once popular, today she is almost forgotten, known primarily to literary antiquarians, that delightful and delighting breed of bookish people who explore the stacks of libraries, finding pleasure in brushing dust off the ghostly, people who are uncritical readers for whom books are not texts buttressing indoctrination, but springs of idiosyncratic enjoyment. Among Meade's books are thirty-odd mysteries. Corpses on the page often endure the passing years better than fictional flesh and blood characters, and Meade's mysteries are feverish with high prices. In the United States a first edition of *The Brotherhood of Kings* (1899) in fine condition is priced at $3,750 plus $10 postage, though I suspect the seller would forgo the mailing charge if a mystery aficionado shoveled up the green. In Britain a first edition of *The Sorceress of the Strand* (1902) is tagged at $1,272 plus $30 postage.

Because I won't pay more than a Hamilton for a volume and won't read books online or reprints published after 1920, I have read neither mystery. Of course, if a devotee of crime who is not suffering from a mental decline sent me copies of the novels published before 1920, I'd read the books. He should know I prefer well-marked copies. If pristine, I promise to decorate them, writing the name of a distinguished graduate of Alcatraz on the end papers. If the day is sunny, maybe I'll laugh and include a bonus, say, a sketch of a jail cell adorned with a partially dug escape hole. Perhaps I'll draw two legs disappearing through the hole. Oh, heck, maybe the prison will be Angola. If that's the case, I'll draw an alligator peering out of the hole, a lady alligator toothy, winsome, and hungry. Until the mysteries arrive, I will continue to read Meade's novels ostensibly for young readers of which she wrote around one hundred and fifty. I have purchased fourteen of her "charming tales for girls," as an advertisement called them. I admire charm. It separates cream from milk. A woman without charm, my friend Josh says, "is sadly but a woman, and a man similarly beggared is a guy or, if he is given to vulgar pretension, a gent. In any case both are viral and should be avoided like steak tartare on a hot day."

I read Meade's novels in bed at night. They relax and banish worry. The tales are school and domestic comedies. Melodrama seasons but does not overpower the stories. Although the lives of the characters don't always flow smoothly, Meade's words never toss topsy-turvy through tale-smashing emotions. Among the characters is Money, a one-dimensional social Janus, present but just as often absent, the effects of which impel plots forward. Money can affect wonders and, of course, disasters. At its best, great wealth enables characters to choose their friends, freeing them from having to grovel to the intrusively "monied." References to God are sometimes made at the conclusion of chapters, at which times "His" will or latitudinarian moral truths serve as periods closing conversations or conscientious dithering.

Most characters are girls, usually members of family nests ranging in age from infants to the newly marriageable. Rarely do the girls have as many brothers as sisters, and most brothers are young, usually unattractive imps. Older brothers are often unintelligently assertive. Sometimes older brothers drift from propriety and become soiled for a signature of pages. They are, however, salvageable, especially when scrubbed by the lily hands of younger sisters. School mistresses are frequently starchy and hidebound. Aunts are oftentimes impatient and cross-grained. Mothers can be sickly, absent, terrible teachers, prone to "nervous storms," and suffering from emotions changeable as a "weathercock." Good mothers know "a child is like a little flower; he wants sunshine, and there is no sunshine like mother love." Poor mothers are unconcerned and too self-centered either to love or offer good advice. Is being rich the "only way to be truly, truly happy?" Sibyl asks Mr. Rochester after talking to her mother. "It is not," Rochester replies then asks, "Who has been putting such an idea into your head?" Fathers are admirable, distant, and decent even if wrong-headed, for example, initially disapproving of "the modern girl," young females with "advanced ideas" who imagine attending Girton or Newnham at Cambridge. Several fathers are impecunious doctors. When fathers die, the oldest girl in the family rises to the educational and moral occasion and becoming "little mother" nurtures her siblings.

Deaths occur frequently. Although they cause confusion and sadness, most are not exceptional, and awareness of and closeness to death seem parts of a natural life. A few deaths are more literary than actual. They occasion palls of bruised, purple prose. Almost always such deaths detail the lugubrious declines of tubercular saints whose wings fledge as rivulets of narrative tears wash away their soiled flesh. A handful of rustics appear. A few are deserving poor. Some are calloused. None are dangerous, and others are colloquial and not to etiquette raised. The beginnings and middles of the novels are rich with story and light-hearted fiddle-faddle. Although the final details are anticipated, endings occur so suddenly they resemble strokes, a fatal matter perhaps for the literary critic but not for the dozing reader who embraces the quick good cheer and doesn't mind stories stopping so he can snap off the lamp on his bedside table. In a way the novels are sleeping tablets. Rarely do they teach. What lessons appear are commonsensical and rarely elicit dissent. When a friend told Leslie that she pitied her because her beauty would lead her into temptation, Leslie replied that her mother taught her to regard "a pleasant and pretty face as a blessing." "Beauty is a power which can be used for good," she said. "If one thinks of it in that way, one need never be vain." The books don't cause nightmarish dreams or awaken foreboding thoughts about duty or accomplishment. On finishing a tale, the reader shuts the volume, drops it onto the floor, stretches, yawns, forgets the plot, and doesn't imagine doing anything.

"The books one reads in childhood," George Orwell wrote, "and perhaps most of all the bad and good bad books create in one's mind a sort of false map of the world, a series of fabulous countries into which one can retreat at odd moments throughout the rest of life." Meade's books for girls similarly create a false map, not only for youthful readers, but also for adults. In Meade's country not everybody lives on "Honeysuckle Farm," but people sing in the sunshine. They forget guns and rapine. No inhabitant has seen a drone or heard of nuclear war. People laugh, and if they believe most politicians to be jackasses, they don't mention the fact at dinner. Unlike Tennessee Republicans they would not have restricted performances of the famous show "The Twelve Dancing Pigs" because the performers were boars in drag wearing tutus with flaming chiffon skirts. Never would they have hired a troop of circus acrobats composed of "little people" to dress as children and crash drag shows. Mrs. Meade's people would have prevented paparazzi from photographing the "children" skipping rope, turning cartwheels, and playing doctor. The girls at Middleton School would have banded together with those from the Great Shirley School and seizing ferules stopped the acrobats from becoming the darlings of social media and of conspiracy theorists claiming "the poor babies" to be visual proof of the insidious magnetism of drag shows. In Meade country people behave better. They do not censure books, fly flags, yell at the radio, lie out of meanness, detest the Good Samaritan, and lust to control the lives of strangers. When they imagine going their ways, they reminisce and envision brighter old places.

How relaxing to enter a living room and instead of observing a blackleg lawyer on television fishing for accident victims see a girl rearrange a flower table that looks "anyhow" and afterward straighten an antimacassar on the back of a "great arm chair" so that the house looks occupied by "Capables" rather than "Incapables." How cheering to see Innocence triumphing over people whose heads are big but whose hearts are small. A reader smiles when "the greatest pride of all, that of absolute ignorance" receives its comeuppance. Perhaps more enjoyable are reliving attic days and sneaking into a "small, stuffy, dusty, dirty" sanctum sanctorum and discovering "three teeth and the bit of a jawbone of a Chinaman who died a thousand years ago."

Seventy-five years ago, I ran bare foot in the sunshine, and in the rain. I hardly noticed the difference. Unlike Olive Latimer's friend Freda, I was too young to be afraid when people said they were happy. My dreams had not proved to be "but early mists of the morning." Then I strolled among "tokens of wealth and prosperity without seeing them." I was simply Sammy. "A long train of noble ancestors" didn't bestow untold advantages, or disadvantages, on me. Moreover, my parents and grandparents were too nice to complicate the plot of a novel. Mr. Inquisitive, who explored the lanes near Meade's Cozy Corner, was a stranger, but every morning when I was young, I saw Master Inquisitive in the looking glass. I didn't find it "disagreeable not to understand people." I was too busy. Like Polly Maybright, I had a collection of grubs and chrysalides. Like Judy and Babs Merton, I "loved" spiders and watched butterflies escaping their "butterfly-cases." Unlike Hal and his little sister Ethel I did not collect birds' eggs. Under my bed I kept the shell of a box turtle. On exhibit atop the windowsill in my room was a collection of paper wasps' nests, and at the back of a drawer in my desk was a small box containing the tails of fence lizards. I did not keep a pet canary named Daffodil in a cage. Never did I remove eggs from a kingfisher's nest as did Ethel's friend George. When I found a bird's egg on the ground, I warmed it beneath a lamp and tried to hatch it.

I was a real boy. If I had lived in Mrs. Meade's fabulous country, I'd have been a lively and wholesome little girl, playful but not fretful and certainly not "a trouble-the-house." I wasn't a rebel like Kathleen O'Hara who called school "purgatory." Even after learning to enjoy lessons, Kathleen was careful not to become a dull "schoolroom child." Students in Mrs. Meade's schools were rarely carefree and often unhappy. Amid the distemper of rules and propriety, secrets rooted, and the goal of producing "accomplished women" often disappeared. Among the girls, conspiracies and betrayals flourished, at least until the novels ended and a Mentholatum of *deus ex machina* words soothed plots and cooled animosities. "A little knockabout Red Rover would have worked miracles quicker," I thought. But Mrs. Meade's schools were private and all the pupils, girls. The grand times of my public schooldays when I ran hard and lovingly at Sarah Ann and when Linda tied my shoes were four decades in the future.

I didn't tell stretchers but would have fashioned a few whoppers if I'd heard Flossie Griffiths call them tarradiddles. Archaic and unfamiliar language and expression have delighted me since childhood. They infuse life into dead thoughts. They make a person see, really see, things and places that have become so weary and well-known they are invisible. Nowadays if an undigestible lecture causes a feminist to suffer from spasms of the diaphragm, I'll urge her to call the ailment she-cups not he-cups. If she attempts to "blow my nose off" and says something unbecoming a lady, I will rise above the glottis, and hoofing up the high medical ground urge her to seek the miraculous benefits of "a course of electricity." Next Wednesday when Vicki and I go to Dog Lane Café I won't embarrass her by requesting the nonexistent "Middle of the Week Cake Price." Instead, I'll order "a thick and a doorstep," on Mrs. Meade's menu coffee and buttered bread, but now as emended by me and Time, coffee and a muffin, a puzzler sure to elicit an interrogative "huh?"

The first chapter of *A Young Mutineer* opened with an epigraph: "Sun and shower—sun and shower—/ Now rough, now smooth, is the winding way; / Thorn and flower—thorn and flower—/ Which will you gather? Who can say?" Mrs. Meade's girls wandered knotty paths. Frequently the correct way forward was weedy and confusing, and sometimes girls took wrong turns and became momentarily lost. Thorns occasioned pain, but briars were sensitive phlebotomists and didn't jab deeply causing blood to pool blue and black under the skin. Occasionally anecdotes hinted that not everyone would cradle a bouquet at eventide. On Hilda's asking her friend Mildred what Babs her little sister was doing, Milly recounted that when she last saw her, Babs was squatting on the floor with a blind, three-day old kitten in her lap. "The kitten squalled frightfully, and Babs kept on calling it 'poor, pretty darling,'" Milly said, adding, "I thought badly of the kitten's future prospects, but well of its nurse's." At the end of *A Bevy of Girls* and after years of selfish behavior, Nesta determined to reform. To do so she had to master her wayward nature and do "a great many hard things." Because she was "full of self-will, pride and obstinacy," the struggle was difficult, and she "found as life went on that she had to go on doing hard things, harder and harder each day." Eventually she subdued the nipping frosts of the wintry side of her nature and the scorching tempests of her violent passions. She owed her success, the last sentence in the book asserted, "to God," a narrative hop, skip, and dodge, and a genuflection so platitudinous that readers, both children and adults, hardly noticed it.

Based on a tenth of Mrs. Meade's novels for girls and only five percent of all her volumes, my descriptions of her stories and characters are more personal than objective. Amid Mrs. Meade's athenaeum of volumes, determined readers can unearth whatever treasure or carrion they anticipate finding. And that's all right. Discovering pages that prove that one's fancies are true is easy and satisfying. But it does not motivate me. How pleasant to be nursed by Dorothy Fraser in *A Girl in Ten Thousand*, and be diverted from the pestiferous machinations of the elected inmates of the "Home for Incapables." What a relief it is to escape the scarlet fever of "news today" and its bacterial accounts of classified documents and celebrations of military adventurism. Unfortunately, I am not able to avoid all news because my friend Josh follows current events. "The problem," Josh said recently, "is not with people who purloin classified papers. All politicians and their hangers-on do so. The problem arises because functionaries classify every scrap of old rag as secret. True democracies are not raised on papyrus foundations of secrecy. If a congressman has a hemorrhoidectomy tomorrow, all details of the operation, including color photos, will be classified."

Avoiding lettered diphtheria is difficult even with the aid of Meade's "lady nurse." Last week before my yearly "Wellness Examination," I received an impertinent questionnaire. Its crudity disturbed my reading about the misadventures of Deb, her doll Lady Caroline, and Flopsy, an aged, stub-tailed, buff-colored English terrier who longed to tell his little mistress how much he admired her. The questionnaire awakened intemperate and unhealthy scorn. Was I depressed and how often? Did I ever think about committing suicide? In the present "Eve of Destruction," only imbeciles are not occasionally depressed. Instead of suicide why not ask what I thought about pets, adultery, or chocolate? I knew that all reactions to my responses would be glib. Did I own a pet because I was anti-social and misanthropic? Had I not committed adultery because I was inhibited or incapable of affection? On the subject of chocolate, what sort of person liked semi-sweet? Did that mean he was incorrigibly trans? Across the top of the form in bright red ink I wrote, "These questions make me want to commit suicide."

Shortly afterward I fed the questionnaire into my paper shredder, an act almost as gratifying as eating a bowl of dark chocolate ice cream. I then resumed reading about Deb. She had just met her only friend, Michael, a little boy with "a bright head of golden red curls." Michael wore a scuffed blouse and was upset because on his refusal to appear scrubbed and wear a suit to greet his absentee mother he was told she wouldn't love him. "If she's that kind, if she only cares for stupid, clean boys in velvet suits," he told Deb, "I'm sorry she is coming home." Deb and Michael were meant for each other, and although only five years old, they decided to get married the following day. "No," I thought, "not the next day but at the end of the book." "Rob & Myrtle" gave *Deb and the Duchess* to "Mr and Mrs. A. J. Hollister." I mulled contacting Myrtle and asking if I was right about the marriage, but I did not know how to reach her or Rob, especially since the novel was published in 1890. I suspected wherever they were was sunny. Meade's girls' books were not for the gloomy of heart, or of soul. Of course, I could have skipped ahead and read the conclusion to the novel. But then I would have missed the pleasures of courtship and the silly doings that make a quiet life glow. I would have missed a platter of evocative associations, some bumpy with nuts, others once bitter but now milky and rich with fantasies of coconut and caramel, maple and mint, still others truffles, magical truffles once stale but now reconstituted and sweet with recollections.

Among the pleasures of reading weary way-worn books is that when a person finishes the last paragraph, shuts the covers, and starts on his way, he often doesn't stride into the present but instead lingers in the literary past of brittle pages, sauntering and ambling loose-limbed and loose-minded. Attached to the ends of Meade's novels often appeared a signature of advertising pages. "There Is Money In Poultry," proclaimed the copy for L. K. Felch's *Poultry Culture*, while "our new possessions," another ad emphasized, made it "imperative" that people purchase "Dictionaries of the Foreign Languages" and learn the German, French, and Spanish equivalents of English words. In general, however, the pages promoted novels. Many of the writers remain familiar: among them, Captain Marryat, Edward Ellis, and Horatio Alger. Others have slipped from sight: Charles Carleton Coffin, Mary J. Holmes, and Rosa Nouchette Carey. Sophia May isn't much read today, but during the last decade several of her forty-five books have been reprinted, predominantly her stories of Miss Prudy. Years ago, in the loft of a barn in Nova Scotia, I found four of May's volumes describing the travels of Dolly Dimple. The books were old, and their pages irresistibly brown and waterlogged. I read them at night in the kitchen sitting close to the wood stove and smiling myself into dimples.

In several of Meade's volumes appeared an advertisement for *Helen's Babies*, "Some Account of Their Ways, Innocent, Crafty, Angelic, Impish, Witching, and Repulsive." First published in the 1870s, the book sold widely for seventy years. In 1929 G. K. Chesterton praised it, saying it was interesting when it appeared "and it is interesting still, even if nobody is interested." In its day it was "one of the most popular books in the world," George Orwell said, judging it "the kind of book that has no literary pretensions, but which remains readable when more serious productions have vanished." "We guarantee that you will not suffer from 'the blues' after reading this book," the advertisement promised. "A book to make me sing in the sunshine and laugh as I go on my way," I thought. Ten days after seeing the ad, I owned an edition printed in 1881. The author John Habberton was a young bachelor, and the book describes ten days Harry, his fictional double, spent caring for his sister Helen's two small boys Budge and Toddie. Aged five and three, the children were holy terrors. Innocent, affectionate, and innately moral, they were also maddingly irresponsible and mischievous. They were in fact and indeed boys' boys, loving and beloved, the sort of children about whom grownups tell stories, simultaneously laughing and shaking their heads in exasperation.

Shortly after Uncle Harry began minding Helen's "best children in the world," Alice Mayton, a girl Harry had long admired from afar, saw the children with their uncle and gushed, "you look as if you have been having such a good time." "If King Herod were yet alive," Harry responded, "I'd volunteer as an executioner, and engage to deliver two interesting corpses as a moment's notice." Between them the boys dropped a kitten down a well, endlessly demanded stories and candy, overdosed on paregoric, ate cigars, cut themselves with shaving razors, climbed on roofs, tormented a goat, and got stung by wasps. Toddie broke into Harry's trunk and tossed the carefully packed contents around like confetti. He did so "because." To me and to sensible adults, Toddie's one-word reply is the best reason conceivable. Boys, and girls, who discover locked trunks, pry the lids up, and delve helter-skelter through the contents, using their arms and hands as shovels, are certain to become buoyant moral adults, tolerant, understanding people, who sympathize with and forgive the foibles of others, in short, superb mommies and daddies. Their offspring will not become "dressed-up drawing-room" dollies. If a child doesn't have access to an attic and trucks stacked like bales of hay, ethical parents should know that closets are adequate formative substitutes, especially those mothy with racks of musty clothes and shoeboxes so akimbo, they tumble like cardboard building blocks leading anybody who opens the door to conclude that during a thunderstorm "from Hell" the floorboards of the house buckled and almost collapsed.

Most stories the babies requested were biblical. Uncle Harry did his best, but age had sapped inspiration from his words and reduced the tales to outlines. Before Harry finished his renditions, Budge usually interrupted and fleshing out his accounts with "the freshness of youth" and "the humors of innocence" made the stories live. After the rain stopped and Noah left the ark, Budge recounted, "he and his little boys and girls went wherever they wanted to, and everything in the world was all theirs; there wasn't anybody to tell 'em to go home, nor no kindergarten schools to go to, no bad boys to fight 'em, nor nothin'. Now tell us 'nother story." Habberton fought in the Civil War, and the best 'nother story described an incident in the war. Just as two opposing calvary troops "took their swords out to kill each other" preparatory to charging down a road, a little boy who had been picking berries for his mother ran across the road. He didn't make it. He caught his toe, fell, and started crying. When both troops reined in their horses, a soldier dismounted, picked up the boy, and began to console him. Next a soldier from the opposing side got off his horse and examined the boy. "Then more soldiers came from both sides to look at him; and when he got better and walked home, the soldiers all rode away, because they didn't feel like fighting just then."

At its best, light literature alleviates the burden of living and brings light, that is, sunshine. On finishing *Helen's Babies* I thought about hailing Mr. Tambourine Man and asking him to play a song for me. But that wasn't necessary. I was and am content in the jingle-jangle days of radiant reading. Of course, I've long been aware of the Carter Family's warning that "the little black train" is "a-coming." But I am not ready to board. On the floor under my chair in the study are three more novels by Mrs. Meade: *Wild Kitty*, *Sweet Nancy*, and *The Children of Wilton Chase*, 'nother stories bound to make me sing and laugh, perchance to dream. When I finish reading them and go on my way, I won't wobble like an old man. I will be steady on my feet and perhaps trip the light, literary toe. I won't leave my armchair, but I'll dance well enough to win an elementary-school Waltz contest. I haven't chosen a partner, but Uncle Harry's sweetheart Alice Mayton is more than a girl on a page. She's too shy for a fallaway, but after I put some flowers in her hair, she will enjoy turns and swirls especially since minding Budge and Toddie absorbs all her fiancé's attention. There won't be a love-in. But maybe we'll be tempted to dance cheek-to-cheek. Because recently I haven't lifted anything heavier than a book, my hands are silky. They aren't blistered and calloused as they were sixty years ago when I rowed, and Carol said holding my hand was like holding a foot.

4

The Pond Is Dry. Part I

In August Vicki and I went to the annual Western Nova Scotia Exhibition, something we have done almost every summer for forty years. In the past the Exhibition was a grand agricultural event, redolent with the fragrance of barnyard and stall, the highlights of which were ox hauls. Times have changed. The wooden barns have been razed, and the hauls exist almost as a postscript taking place on Saturday night outside in the dark. A brick building has replaced the main hall. Among other things, it hosts Yarmouth's minor league ice hockey team. During Exhibition week, sundry shows took place on the rink. Step dancers clacked and swayed; country music singers strummed guitars, and around his head a juggler tossed chain saws buzzing like hornets. For Vicki and me, the pinnacle of the day and maybe the summer was an afternoon of professional wrestling. Some two hundred and fifty people attended. Many were simple and believed the matches real. Vicki and I sat at ringside on folding chairs and had a grand time. We cheered the heroes and booed the villains. We drank Pepsi Colas and ate "Montreal Sausages" awash with mustard and buried under palls of onions. Midway through the afternoon, a wrestler stopped yanking his opponent about by the hair, leaned over the ropes, and addressed me. "Don't laugh so hard, old-timer," he said. "You might have a heart attack." "What?" I said to Vicki. "Old-timer! The poor man is almost blind. He shouldn't be allowed to continue until after he has been to the eye doctor."

Vicki and I spent eleven weeks in Nova Scotia this past summer. Aside from a dormitory of red squirrels and granaries of granola-manufacturing mice, Four Winds, our rambling old Gothic Revival house, had been empty for thirty-four months. Decades ago, a reviewer said that I wrote the books Thoreau might have written had he married and fathered children. Since then, I've imagined writing a family man's version of *Walden Pond*. For the past fifty years Thoreau has been a presence on my pages. I wrote a lengthy introduction to *Walden* and several articles about naturalists, his predecessors and followers: Gilbert White, John Burroughs, Charles Conrad Abbott, and William Hamilton Gibson, among guidebooks of others. I wrote signatures of pages describing the forty acres of wood and bog, meadow and shoreline surrounding Four Winds. I overdosed on wildflowers and mushrooms, trees, lichens, sedges, shorebirds, reptiles, and insects of all kinds: moths, butterflies, beetles, caterpillars, and spiders among troves of others. I followed porcupines through woods and stalked short-tailed weasels along stone walls. Early in the morning I sat on the side porch and listened to the bubbling serenade of a sparrow in a willow. I roamed the green and creaturely world, and every June before driving to Nova Scotia I planned to write my *Walden*. I never wrote the book because living itself distracted me. To emend Thoreau's often-quoted words, living sucked the leisure out of days. I didn't live deep, but I imagined I did so. Life was too various to be driven into a corner, too richly diverse to be reduced to an economist's "lowest terms."

In 1899 Elizabeth Von Arnim's *The Solitary Summer* was published. "I want to be alone for a whole summer and get to the very dregs of life," she explained, paraphrasing Thoreau. "I want to be as idle as I can, so that my soul may have room to grow." At summer's end when asked if her soul grew, she answered "not a bit." Plans go astray when one has a family and when a person must remove dust covers from the furniture in nine rooms and take down wooden shutters. Splitting firewood shatters well-wrought maxims as do scrubbing, sweeping, hanging, and carting—stocking a house for the familial. Thoreau was domestically naïve and inexperienced. He was wrong. Such duties don't smother a man and mark a "fool's life." Instead, they reveal loving responsibility. Like all earthly matters, they are evanescent and will inevitably be corrupted by moth and rust. They will disappear amid the compost of Time. Nevertheless, they are the real gold of family living. To the elderly, Thoreau's "simplicity, simplicity, simplicity" seems a lament, the cry of loneliness, not an exhortation to reform one's life.

Details don't fritter existence away; they enrich it. What is left after the essentials and inessentials vanish? What life does a person have when he is warehoused in assisted living and no longer capable of assisting others? "How many a poor immortal soul have I met well nigh crushed," Thoreau wrote, "creeping down the road of life, pushing before it a barn seventy-five feet by forty." At Four Winds, the barn joins a backhouse. In turn the backhouse joins the big house with its two pantries, three parlors, five bedrooms, two long halls, a radically steep fourteen-step stairway, and a country kitchen in which cooking is done on a wood-burning iron stove. A range cannot be installed because the wiring dates from the 1950s and has been out of code so long that it is antediluvian. Our water comes from a deep artesian well. The water is good for cleaning and for most cooking but cannot be drunk because it contains more iron than the armor on the front of a Sherman tank. While listing details, I should add that we did not have internet or a television. Our radio was thirty-five years old and only picked up three stations clearly, one of which played mind-hemorrhaging pop music. Moreover, a decade ago Nova Scotia decided that only year-round residents were entitled to mailboxes. Consequently, none of our mail was forwarded from Connecticut. Early in the summer the phone was connected. In our eleven weeks it rang four times. Robocrooks made the initial two calls. The other two came from our son Francis informing us that Storrs was so dry the yard did not need mowing. Vicki brought a cellphone to the house and during the summer struggled to learn to use it. She was successful enough to be confused.

Thoreau spent two years and two months at Walden Pond, leaving in 1847 when he was thirty years old. *Walden* was published seven years later. I have spent more than six years of summer months in Nova Scotia beginning when I was thirty-nine. Thoreau said he went to Walden "to transact some private business with the fewest obstacles." Only rarely have Vicki and I been by ourselves at Four Winds. If the natural occurrences of summertime living and owning a hundred-and-sixty-year-old house can be ruled out—fallen trees, collapsed ceilings, crumpled sheds, leaky roofs and windows, stolen pipes, moribund pumps, a barn twisted off its foundation by a hurricane—we have experienced few obstacles. What has filled summers is the married person's business, family. Our Walden has been a richly cluttered, populous place. We went to Four Winds not to drive life into a corner or put to rout "all that was not life." "Living is so dear." I didn't plot hammering expectations into words. I was curious and appreciative, and instead of shaving close, I relished the weedy and untrimmed. My "true account" is that of a wobbly eighty-one-year-old husband and father, the meandering loosely formed thoughts of a sunny pessimist who loved domestic life, the writing of a person who actually sucked "out the marrow of life."

"Old deeds for old people," Thoreau wrote. Family hours for family people. Vicki spent the first week after our arrival cleaning, stocking, and hanging pictures and curtains. She decorated the rooms with bibelot collected during previous summers. These transformed an unheated, seasonal vacation house into a home, awakening associations warm with recollection and hopeful expectation. Vicki got up before dawn and went to bed long after midnight. My days were easier. I piddled about outside, trying to stay out of Vicki's way and aware that no one would notice what I did or neglected to do. I sawed fallen limbs, trimmed bushes, chopped Japanese knotweed, and pulled bales of Virginia creeper. When Vicki's nerves frayed, I retreated to the barn and split wood. On the eighth day after we opened the house, Edward arrived. Against my wishes he drove from South Carolina and, after spending two nights in Storrs, took the ferry from Bar Harbor to Yarmouth as Vicki and I had done. With him he bought Bea, his seventy-pound Old English Bulldog. Bea was good-natured, but only two years old and rompingly high with energy, not a companion for our three rescue dogs, the youngest of which was fourteen, the heaviest Suzie at twelve pounds, the lightest Mee at seven. After spending two days at Four Winds, Edward drove to Halifax and fetched Erica his wife and Sammy their eighteen-month-old boy from the airport. Sammy was a delight, but he was as rambunctious as Bea. Edward and family stayed a fortnight. Near the end of their visit, Eliza flew in from

California and stayed two weeks. Eliza is a vegetarian, practically a vegan, a diet good for the body and probably one's psyche, but hard on the cook preparing meals. Shortly after Eliza went back to California, Vicki's brother Geoff came for nine days. Just before Geoff returned to New York, Francis arrived for a fifteen-day stay.

Vicki made nut loaves for Eliza, but in any case we ate meat rarely. Fish was dear, and the only seafood we ate at home was in a chowder Vicki bought at Sobeys in Yarmouth or in tuna sandwiches she prepared for picnics on the beach. Once a week Vicki cooked a meat patty, and she concocted salads. At practically every meal we had vegetables: beets and beet greens, Swiss chard, carrots, peas, snap beans, and potatoes. Although corn was in season, we didn't eat it. The stove is small, and Vicki believed bringing a big pot to boil for corn would destroy the firebox. For desserts we generally had berries from our fields, local strawberries, and Vicki's rhubarb flummery. In past summers rhubarb grew beside a stone wall in Ma's property, the south field. During our absence it disappeared, smothered by bay and ferns. Thoreau left Walden explaining that he had other lives to live. In life everything is fleeting. In the country, however, evanescence is especially apparent. Change forces a person to live other lives. Vicki bought rhubarb at the Farmer's Market. The paths I blazed through the woods at Four Winds in previous summers were overgrown, and great portions of the woods themselves had become impassable and almost unrecognizable. Spruce had rotted and toppled. And I? Well, I hadn't fallen, but I was leaning, my top branches caught in and supported by family, other trees, and doctors.

When "a lady" offered him a mat, Thoreau turned it down, saying he preferred to wipe his feet on the sod before the door, adding that it was best to avoid "the beginnings of evil." At Four Winds doors were open all day. To have closed them would have been the beginning of real, not fanciful evil. Yet, there were times I was so tired I imagined getting away. Later, of course, I realized that I'd left Connecticut and was already away. To be alive is to be inconsistent. On other occasions, I lamented Vicki's and my middle-class means. By making distance possible, relative plenty often shatters families and indirectly wrings tangible love out of days. It undermines small community and begets loneliness. Our children attended colleges that exposed them to the seduction of possibility and the allure of the faraway. The schools may have been good for them, but they weren't good for Vicki and me. They were cruel. The children are admirable adults, but they don't live around the corner. Vicki cannot shop at Price Chopper with Eliza or rub little Sammy's head. Neither Edward nor Francis can help me plant iris or rake leaves. We can't be together. We can enjoy frenetic visits during the summer or holidays, but we can't be a family relishing the unnoticeable and the unremarked.

Thoreau described his days metaphorically rather than accurately. Being a recluse was a convenient fiction. He went to Concord practically every day. Vicki and I also left the house frequently. Some forty afternoons we drove five miles to Salmon River. At D. J.'s Corner Store and Café, we drank coffee and ate fudge cake in hopes of invigorating ourselves. Occasionally family members accompanied us and ate ice cream cones, flavors with pancreas-bruising names like Hoof Prints, Bubblegum, Moon Mist, and Dinosaur Bones. On Sunday Vicki and I breakfasted at D. J.'s, always on coffee, two eggs over medium, crispy bacon, and toasted homemade white bread. We chatted with the owners' twin daughters Lurelle and Lisanne. In fact, I talked to everyone in the store, no matter what they were eating or what they had purchased. On our last visit Dorothy, who managed the cash register, treated us to coffee and said she hoped we'd return "next summer."

Several times every week we drove twelve miles to Yarmouth, and I borrowed books from the town library. Friday was shopping day, the schedule crammed with trips to Milton Laundromat, Walmart, Bulk Barn, Red and White grocery in Dayton, and Canadian Tire. On Saturday we returned to Yarmouth for the farmer's market. When family took the ferry back to Bar Harbor, we drove to Cape Forchu and waved at the ship as it sailed past. On all excursions to Yarmouth, we stopped at Tim Hortons. We had coffee and a muffin or a breakfast sandwich. Regulars called me "Buddy," and I chatted with Biscuit the cleaning woman. Most of the regulars had grown up in Yarmouth, and sometimes Vicki and I sat with them. Bubbles got her nickname in elementary school, the source her cheery nature, not a career as an exotic dancer. Yarmouth is a French fry town, and outside the house we rarely ate a full meal. When we did, I had fried clams seasoned with overheard conversations. "How are you doing?" an elderly man said to a grizzled fellow his age in line in Wendy's. "Staying out of trouble," the second man replied. "Yeah?" the first man said. "Yeah, it's a fulltime job; let me tell you," the man responded. "Yeah," the first man said, nodding his head.

Our jaunts did not evoke pithy or didactic observations. I didn't ponder missing life. Tires on the Subaru were four years old, and I worried about a flat on an isolated country road. Hurricane Dorian peeled shingles off our barn. The barn had been repaired, but I fretted about a roofing nail's going walkabout and puncturing a tire if I parked close to the house. Excursions like that to wrestling were our sedate version of honky-tonking. We did not wish to "practice resignation" and "live meanly," couped inside our "cabin." We didn't try to elevate life but simply enjoy it. Every August the Coal Shed Music Festival occurs on the waterfront in Yarmouth. For three weekends musicians perform in an open tent. Performances are free, and the audience swells and shrinks as people wander in and out and through days. Much of the music is a familiar mix of gospel and country: "The Wreck of Old 97," "Billy in the Low Ground," "Will the Circle Be Unbroken," and "I Saw the Light." This year singers assured listeners that the Blue Moon of Kentucky was shining and Jimmy Brown hadn't gone to college and was still a newsboy. Men wearing scuffed shoes were pleased to learn that the Chattanooga shoeshine boy remained at work, popping his boogie woogie rag. Moreover, singers predicted that the girl who forsook her penniless admirer and married wealth would eventually see the new wear off her chrystal chandelier. They noted that on another road an abandoned but ever-hopeful lover left the key in the mailbox. One sad woman lamented that she "was a walking, talking, crying, barely-breathing broken heart." However, she was better off than the dying gal who urged her lover to plant "a little bunch" of flowers by her grave. She wasn't a horticulturalist. The variety didn't matter. All that counted was the "hand" that planted them.

Strangers sat beside one another in the tent and chatted. Late one Friday a man near Vicki offered to buy us sodas. The offer unlocked conversation. The man said he was eighty-two, a stripling compared to his father who was 112 years old. Longevity was a family trait as the father's two brothers were 106 and 102. Luck also ran in the family. Several years ago in the Ontario lottery, the man's father won 18 million dollars. "He gave me nine million," the man recounted. "I bought seven houses. In them live abandoned children. I buy their food and clothes and make sure they go to school." "What a story," Vicki said after we left the festival. "Yes," I said, "a real whopper. None of it is true, but don't you wish it were?" Fiction seasons the lives of most people, certainly mine. "We are not a nation of truth-lovers," as Hunter S. Thompson put it fifty years ago. The next day Vicki and I returned to the festival. Our philanthropist's stories had rooted and spread. The father's winnings had grown to 28 million dollars. The man still possessed the seven houses, but in addition he owned two fleets, one of fishing boats, the other of tractor trailers. The man's autobiography fell on receptive ground. Like some of the sentimental music played at the festival, his accounts brightened moments. As people discussed him, they smiled. For a little while they marveled at and perhaps appreciated not the man, but man himself. "Weren't those tales something, Buddy?" a fellow spectator said to me. "They sure were," I said.

"Music begats hunger in most capitals, and the cafes of Paris are never so full as after a great night at the opera," Captain Rotherby opined at the beginning of E. Phillips Oppenheim's *The Lost Ambassador*. 90 Water Street in Yarmouth isn't Paris's 9th arrondissement, and even after a hefty seasoning of "Good Lookin's" home cooking, "Your Cheatin' Heart" is not quite as appealing as Anna Moffo's *Manon*. Nevertheless, Rotherby had it right. After a musical afternoon at the Coal Shed, Vicki and I headed for The Dinner Plate and a platter of fried clams and local champagne, that is, a couple of flutes of Rusty Truck Red Ale.

Our honky-tonking featured more honks than clanging tonks. In mid-summer the Seafest took place in Yarmouth. It lasted a week and a half and was parochial and neighborly with a yard sale at the Yarmouth County Museum, a scavenger hunt for children, and a kite-flying contest. On the first Saturday, Run Nova Scotia "presented" the Sheila Poole ten-kilometer road race. I ran the race more than twenty times. Alas, my racing days had ended. As Montaigne put it, "I have seen the leaves, the blossoms, and the fruit, and now I see the tree withered." Well, perhaps, not quite—a few galls still malinger. "What's wrong with me?" I said to Vicki bemoaning missing the race. "There's nothing wrong with you except white socks. In the future wear beige," she replied. Vicki's conversation is often lively. Recently after an odd remark I urged her to "be normal." "I'm not quite in a normal mood," she replied. Be that as it may, on the way back to Four Winds from the Seafest, Vicki detoured around Cedar Lake tracing the eight-mile circuit I once ran every day. The greatest change was in me not the countryside. The usual family of ruffed grouse scooted across a ditch. Goldfinches still blew through the thistles beyond the shoulder of the road, and next to Mr. Ellis's barn, geriatric tractors continued sinking off their axles, their fuel tanks liver-spotted and rusty with squamous cells. "What are you thinking about?" Vicki asked when we reached Four Winds. "You look pensive." "A line from Norman Douglas's *Old Calabria*," I said. "As for Manfredonia—it is a sad little place, when the south wind moans and the mountains are veiled in mists."

For most of Seafest Saturday, Main Street was blocked off as the Roaring Twenties Antique Automobile Club sponsored a car show. Parked on Main and along side streets were several hundred old cars and trucks. Owners brought them from all over Atlantic Canada and New England, even from Ohio and Michigan. Edward and I studied vehicles and the stir of people for ninety minutes. I'm not mechanical. Chassis and drive shafts drifted quickly from mind. Instead, I remembered words printed on shirts: "Y Grow Up?" "I Scare Myself," and "Bad to the Bone." Catchphrases appeared on many shirts, the sorts of statements that decorate bumper stickers and pass for wit among dullards, "I Don't Need Google. My Wife Knows Everything" and "I Speak Fluent Sarcasm." Today, slogans reveal more about a person's caste than his job or education. Inside a heart sketched on a short worn by a mild-looking man was "I Enjoy Romantic Walks Through The Garage." On the shirt of a man so musclebound that he could not walk around people but instead shouldered them out of his lane was, "I Don't Give A Damn." A gang of friends wore black T-shirts. Scrawling across the chests in cursive was "Team Asshole." "Clearly accurate," Edward said. Taped to the inside of the rear window of a partially restored 1934 Chevrolet was a sign written in black with a marking pen, "I'm Speeding Because I Have to Poop."

Before leaving Main Street, I bought cups of ice cream for Edward and me. Coiling around the left arm of the man ahead at the counter was a tattoo of a rattlesnake. The snake slithered under the man's T-shirt and reappeared on his throat. The snake was agitated. It circled the man's neck once then reared up, its mouth wide and fangs spitting venom. "Did you notice the snake?" I said to the woman serving ice cream. "Yes," she said. "They are so common there must be a den of rattlesnakes outside town," I said. "Maybe," the woman said, "I've seen a few tattoos of them." "Have you ever seen a tattoo of a garter snake?" I asked holding Edward's and my ice cream. "They are not good body climbers and don't make colorful neckties." "Huh?" the woman responded. "Come on, Dad," Edward said taking my arm.

The following Sunday Vicki and I went to the stock car races seven miles away at Lake Doucette Motor Speedway. Three hundred people attended, and in some races only six cars ran. To spare our backs, Vicki and I sat in the top row of the small grandstand and leaned against a wooden railing. Vicki brought a picnic of cherries, moldy grapes, Coca Colas, and two bags of potato chips, one ketchup flavored, the other lobster. Their sell dates had expired, and the chips were stale. I sat beside a wraith of a man. Next to him was his girlfriend. She looked like a pillow. He was abstemious, but she ate two hamburgers and a platter of fried onion rings. Between races we talked about pickup trucks. My companion was proud of his Ford F-150 and couldn't believe I'd never sat in a pickup. Insofar as the races were concerned, all the cars appeared in several races, and I rooted for number 42, a green and yellow sedan, advertising "Fish Man." Vicki and I enjoyed the races, but we left early before the afternoon cooled. On the way out I stopped at the porta-potty pavilion. Three or four people stood in line before each lavatory. Like a mythological sea, they parted when I joined them. "Let the old guy go first," a middle-aged man said. "Damn," I said to Vicki later as we left the parking lot. "Don't worry about it. On the way home we'll stop at D. J.'s and get ice cream cones." Outside D. J.'s I talked to a motor cyclist setting out for Ontario. Accompanying him in a sidecar was Billy, a small brown dog. "He's travelled almost 300,000 kilometers with me," the man said. "I've never ridden a motorcycle," I said. "What!" the man said. "Hop in the sidecar. Your wife can watch Billy, and I'll take you for a ride."

At Cape Forchu Vicki and I ate blueberry scones in the tea shop then wandered the headland. When the children were young, I scrambled over the volcanic rock as if I were a tree frog with adhesive pads on my toes. Age, pills, and radiation have slowed me. Moreover, I have an arthritic knee. In Connecticut a doctor shot it full of hyaluronic acid or rooster comb to ease the pain. The injection reduced my limp, but afterward I did not spread my arms, bob my head, and cackle. At Forchu a cormorant perched atop an outcrop, but I didn't mistake her for "my black hen" and hop and flap my way into notice. Instead, I pasted my shoes to the ground and looked at flowers blooming in safe, flatland abundance: wild parsnip, pineapple weed, purple and Canada thistle, perfumeries of rugosa roses, white and yellow clover, wild radish, yarrow, dock, beach pea, seaside goldenrod its leaves pursy and gleaming, and sow thistle, the yellow blossoms in star-like profusion and glowing like constellations.

Old people compose more lists than the young. Their records are not confined to groceries or chores. They include great varieties of things like the flowers at Cape Forchu. No one who reaches doctors' appointment years escapes tallying medicines. Emails and telephone calls demand them, and printed copies unlock examination rooms. Metoprolol, Warfarin, Lupron, Atorvastatin, Amlodipine, Losartan, and Levothyroxine—the elderly usually "know not what they do." All have side effects, the most noticeable being that old timers become addicted to lists and making them becomes a sedentary activity and a form of living. Hanging on a rack at D. J.'s store was a forest of "Little Trees," the deodorants one spots hanging from the rearview mirrors of pickup trucks and old sedans, for the record never from new SUV's. The trees came in a great variety of soft and hardwood scents, many resulting from improbable grafts: Summer Linen, Peachy Peach, Bubble Gum, Cotton Candy, Black Ice, Pure Steel, Pina Colada, Dragon Fruit, True North, and Bayside Breeze amid a miniature lumber mill of others. At Bulk Barn, I recorded flours milled from lupin, quinoa, brown rice, white rice, yellow corn, coconut, millet, arrowroot, and teff. Cans of loose tea lined the back of the butcher block table in the kitchen at Four Winds. Each can once held 100 grams of Twinings tea. Now the contents came from the English Tea Store, among them, the Breakfasts, English, Irish, and Scottish; Lapsang Souchong, Russian Caravan, Yorkshire Harrogate, Lady Londonberry, and Buckingham Palace Garden Party. Reading the names didn't transport me to the Island of Apples where Excalibur was forged or to the Paradise of Birds in the sky above which feathers curved in garish rainbows. The songs of the birds were silent but fragrant with ambrosial perfumes. Occasionally a sip of tea swept me near mythical Thule, the shores of which lay beyond the reach of everything, except imagination.

If the "lady" had offered Thoreau a penny rather than a door mat, I wonder if he would have spurned it. I would have quickly accepted it. Pennies form the template on rectangular mats sewn from scraps, usually wool or felt, popular at the end of the nineteenth century. A typical pattern consisted of rows of circles stretching across and down the mat. Within each circle appeared seven smaller circles, each the size of a penny. Mats served as runners and covers. "Perfect," I thought, for the Victorian dresser in Eliza's bedroom, itself known as the Rose Room because bouquets of pink roses decorate the wallpaper. For years I have searched fruitlessly for a penny mat. *Walden* is a marvelous sermon, but worshippers of a certain age only spend one day a week in church. During the six other days, they spend time pursuing unnecessaries like penny mats. On two Saturdays Vicki and I drove to Annapolis Royal. Both times we meandered along George Street and the Annapolis River. The first Saturday was Natal Day. American soldiers attempted to capture Fort Anne and failed for the 9th time in my memory. We visited the Historic Gardens. Most roses had blown, but the marsh across the Allains River exhaled sunshine. Sauntering through the farmers' market was, and has been, the highlight of visits to Annapolis Royal. I ate my way along rows of stalls, my favorite edible a gooseberry Danish. Gooseberries once grew beside a stone wall at Four Winds, but they disappeared under a hedge of smothering bay. While I ate the Danish, a man shouldering a cross strode by chanting "repent." Painted on the cross was "Is Jesus in Your Life?" Attached to the base of the cross was a wheel lessening the burden of carrying it. "Religion lite," a man standing near me said.

The main purpose of the trip was commercial, not dietary or theological. We went to Annapolis to buy gifts at Lucky Rabbit pottery. In past summers we bought a kiln of souvenirs. On the windowsill of my study in Storrs sits a cookie jar, nine inches tall and adorned with sweeps of blue chicory blossoms. Sitting atop the jar is a fat mouse, the only mouse in the house who need not fear a trap. Elsewhere are bowls, bright with goldfinches and cups shadowy with crows. On a display rack atop a battered country chest is a white flounder. Fifteen inches long and ten wide, the fish bristles with fins. Atop its upper surface are yellow tulips and long creepers of partridgeberry. The flounder's eyes, mouth, and spine are porcelain knobs. The bulges prevent resting a tea coaster atop it. For Thoreau, the fish would be an inedible foolish catch. For me, landing the flounder was fun. Vicki's and my purchases are not "hindrances," they are sources of conversation. They invigorate curiosity and spur us into meandering. Eventually they age into memorabilia and maybe into, in Thoreau's words, "pretty toys." But they don't distract from "serious things." The days when I devoted hours to serious matters are behind me. Happily, the toys distract me from lamenting diminishment, that in myself and in the world around me.

At Lucky Rabbit Vicki bought a curio cabinet of bowls, presents for display, not practical kitchen use. On two of the bowls warblers darted through a conservatory of plants, all the plants hybrid, part rainforest and part country field. On another bowl a squid turned pink and hid herself amid kelp and Irish moss. Discounting his labor, Thoreau spent twenty-eight dollars and twelve and a half cents building his house. People like to imagine themselves individuals. How dreadful to reach eighty and realize that one is such a conformist that his years have been unspeakably pedestrian. I won't reveal what Vicki paid for the bowls. The price embarrasses the part of me that believes mentioning the cost of a non-utilitarian object is distasteful, especially if the amount is high. All I will admit is that for the price of the bowls Thoreau could have built a garden suburb, all the houses with indoor plumbing and running water, outside deer-resistant boxwood and holly, redbuds and magnolias. From Vicki and me, our children inherited both the inclination to avoid "higher latitudes" and the hankering to spend gelt and time upon pleasing inessentials.

Francis missed the trips to Annapolis Royal. But once in Beaver River he explored curiosity shops. He purchased a box of bagatelles. Among them was a pair of fifty-year-old cobra-shaped brass candle holders. The holders were eight inches tall.

Near the top, the holders opened into hoods. Above were the capitals. Below the stems, the bases spread in writhing but stable fifteen-inch coils. "For that special dinner," Francis said. However, Francis's prize was a bronze depicting Baron Munchausen riding in a two-wheeled cart. Harnessed to the front of the cart was Brownie, the Baron's horse. In the traditional story during the Baron's journey, a wolf devoured Brownie. The wolf began his meal at Brownie's tail and munched forward, so that on the Baron's reaching his destination, he discovered "a wolf in a horse's skin" had pulled the cart. On the bronze from the withers over the croup and down to the fetlock, the creature was Canis lupus. Forward from the withers over the neck and muzzle, it was all horse. In eleventh grade I wrote an essay about the tale. I said it was portellingly metaphoric. Seeing the bronze brought my paper to mind. Children, I argued seventy years ago, were not usually led astray by uncontrollable emotions and thoughts. However, after they became adults, many people changed. Desire slipped the reins of reason and morality, and while outward appearances remained relatively constant, inwardly some people became brutish and developed unconscionable, wolfish appetites.

Rarely do I purchase items for myself, but I am not a puritanical advocate of "simplify, simplify." Port Maitland is four miles from Beaver River. In the center of the village is the Yellow Barn, a crumbling building into which Rick has crammed, and dumped, the miscellaneous contents of scores of attics. For ten dollars, seven and a half American, I bought a pair of white Sandland Hanley Staffordshire kittens. Four inches tall, blotched with red, and with thin hairless tails, they sat on their haunches looking self-satisfied. Around each of their necks was a gold collar on which hung a loose floppy bow. The kittens probably left the kiln in the 1980s. They lacked pedigrees and were feral, but when I saw them, I smiled. I have since domesticated them. I put them in the living room beside Bob, an orange blown glass snail that Eliza purchased at a craft show in San Francisco. Eliza brought Bob to Nova Scotia and gave him to me as a present. "For the mollusk corner of the mantle," she said.

In *Walden* Thoreau testified that he "never read any memorable news in a newspaper." In Storrs I subscribe to *The Chronicle*, a local daily paper twelve pages long. I ignore the features and read the obituaries. Usually, they describe the lives of strangers, and I am disappointed and regretful that I know so few people. Familiar faces in obituaries are uppers. "Loss of memory is normal," James Hilton wrote in *Random Harvest.* "We all forget things and are equally likely to be reminded of them long after we think they have been forgotten for good." Bathing in water in which a cadaver has been washed does not heal abscesses. But corpses work miracles. They exhume memories and often raise the dead. News of a friend's demise often enlivens my day. I recall the past and smile, not weep. Momentary grief vanishes, and I am gleeful amid recollections of yesteryears. Thoreau described the present in order to shape a better future. I describe the present both in hopes of enjoying moments for themselves and of recalling the forgotten. Sometimes, of course, the past is a haven which shelters one from the immediate. Although Four Winds sits on land above the Gulf of Maine, and the beach below is broad and beautiful, Vicki and I did not walk the beach until our sixteenth day in Beaver River. Chores bound us to the house. When we eventually walked to Black Point, a mile away, I lagged, stumbling down the bluff to the water then limping along the shore. Four years ago, I scampered through breaking waves. Now I trembled as I picked a way through stones above high tide. Although Vicki paused frequently so I could catch her, I trailed. "Forty-five years ago," she said one evening, "I never imagined I'd be married to an old man."

Change of place no longer radically affects me. At eighty, ailments, not ideas or location, alter living. Every weekend Vicki purchased the *Chronicle Herald*, the Halifax newspaper. As in Connecticut, I ignored features and read obituaries. Because of the death of the Queen of England, I read carefully. Avoiding accounts of the Queen's funeral was impossible. Local radio stations metamorphosized into pallbearers of the air. The funereal doings were grotesquely long and emotionally consumptive. Amid the pomp and meretricious vulgarity, the woman's life disappeared. In "Death is a Door," Nancy Byrd Turner wrote, "Death is only an old door / Set in a garden wall; / On gentle hinges it gives, at dusk / When the thrushes call." More appealing to me were people buried in shrouds of revealing words than those embalmed out of personality. I do not know the mainspring of admiration, but I'd rather meet a person who made peach preserves sweet with summer than someone who ruled a nation. How nice it would be to meet Kate who planted a vegetable garden at 96, Jonah famous for his pickles, and Sally known for her green beans. According to the *Herald*, no family member ever left Granny Bess's house without a heart full of love and a pocket full of jellybeans. Also, Joan arranged teacups and saucers on her dining room table. Next to each setting she placed a personal note inviting that person to relax, "sip a cup of tea" then stroll through her garden and smell the flowers. Several people composed their obituaries. Alice announced that she had been cremated, and her ashes divided, a third mailed to her son who lived in Montana, a third buried in Halifax beside those of her late husband, and the remainder sent to a family plot in Luxemburg, her birthplace. While Walter labeled his life a journey which "I will not soon forget," Darlene advertised her book assuring purchasers that proceeds would be donated to a Refugee Center in New Glasgow. Advertisements buried in obituaries don't reach large audiences. Family and two or three dutiful friends will be the only people who buy Darlene's book. They'll display it on a coffee table for a weekend, but they won't read beyond the title page. Rarely are books composed at the end of a person's tablet celebrated for deathless prose. "Only a quiet door in an old wall," Nancy Turner concluded. "Beyond the lintel are green leaves, / Beyond, the light lies still; / Very willing and weary feet / Go over that sill."

Thoreau urged people to read "the best that is in literature." He preached studying the classics and asked, "how many a man has dated a new era in his life from the reading of a book." Ahead of me stretch months of old age, not the possibility of a great awakening or a vital new era. Come spring an octogenarian may get a shroud. But he won't resemble Tennyson's lapwing and get a new crest. Books that appeal to ambitious people in the adolescence and middle age of their lives rarely attract those in their wintry dotage. I have aged beyond the ferule, the pulpit, and Thoreau's ardent sermonizing. In Nova Scotia my reading reflected the happenstance of life. I borrowed a few books from the Yarmouth Library. Often, I was in a hurry, and the appearance of book jackets determined the selections. I also rummaged the house unearthing volumes overlooked in previous summers. Sometimes I read in bed at night, but usually I read in a front parlor, my feet on a poof and the rest of me settling like silt into an armchair sunken off its springs. Beside me stood a table, the legs of which were so warped they trembled and looked like they suffered from rickets. On the table I set pots of tea. Stains from innumerable spills flowed across its surface shimmering like sand ripples. On the mantle across the room a gothic steeple clock ticked rhythmically. Unlike a digital clock, the flashing of which jars and signals Time passing and lost, the clock marked Time's not passing. Its almost unnoticeable sound was a lulling assurance that amid the abrasive fret of living airy continuance endured, its moments inconsequential and thus relaxing and beguiling.

In past summers I read libraries of detective novels. The books may have appealed to me because although teaching was routine, the months ahead were themselves mysterious. Imagining came easily. I mulled traveling to unfamiliar places and experiencing unknowns, these never clear enough to become actual. At eighty, the future was not enigmatic. Instead of fiction, it was nonfiction, as brisk as a health chart or a doctor's prescription pad. Be that explanation as it may or as it may not be, I read comparatively few mysteries. I did not renew my acquaintance with Nero Wolfe, Inspector Grant, or Jack (Flash) Casey. I no longer drink wine, and after decades of wandering Edinburgh with Ian Rankin's John Rebus, the inspector became too bibulous for my temperate palate, and life. He was old enough to have reformed.

I read two of Michael Palmer's novels, but they were so murderous that after closing them I felt like I needed a transfusion before lifting myself out of the armchair. After I read *Resistant*, the early sunlight that shined pink through the low mist over our hay fields no longer seemed light and dreamy with the promise of happy brightness. Instead, it appeared stained by blood splatters. Across the blueberry field lichens swaddling black spruce gleamed for a moment like soiled snow before freezing into ice and vanishing. After stumbling through morgues of corpses, I thought the limbs cadaverous, and my eyes did not leap in joy. As a person shoulders heavier burdens of years, does his capacity for literary appreciation shrink while he simultaneously becomes more sensitive? Answers to questions about "universal noveldom" are best left to critics inexperienced and passionate enough to believe they can live "earnestly" and explicate existence.

Among the pleasures of reading is finding or creating traces of the self. *A Game of Fear* was the 24th Inspector Rutledge mystery written by Charles Todd. In most of the novels Todd was a mother and son pair. I'd followed Rutledge across Great Britain through several summers and would not have read *A Game* had I not noticed the dedication. "This book is especially for Sammy. His endless energy and capacity for love was a comfort for those who knew him. Sammy was the light of his home and all those who lived with him. Dogs, cats, and people will miss him desperately." Unlike me, this Sammy was four-legged. "A slight difference," I told Vicki. "We don't wag our tails the same way, but in many things in addition to names, we are similar." "Oh, Lord!" Vicki exclaimed after which she paraphrased Marcus Aurelius. "Cast away the thirst after books so that your family won't murmur through your final days and will greet your death with weeping and the gnashing of teeth rather than relief."

In Philip MacDonald's *The Rasp*, correspondences between the hero Anthony Gethryn, an amateur sleuth, and me were both closer and further apart than those between good-hearted Sammy and me. Gethryn was the son of a hunting country gentleman "of the old type, who was one of the most brilliant mathematicians of his day." His mother was "a Spanish lady" from an "impoverished and exiled family." Before she married Gethryn's father, she had been a governess, dancer, mannequin, actress, and portrait painter. Similarities are in the eye of the reader. My father came from the country, but he didn't fancy addition and subtraction. The books he read were not bound in leather and adorned with gilt. He wasn't a sportsman and didn't shoot waterfowl with a Winchester Model 12 shotgun. Every morning he rode a bus downtown where he worked for an insurance company for forty-five years. Mother always fit in and was never an exile. She was a dead shot and a fine horse woman, both of which she forswore after marrying Father. She didn't paint but went one better and had my portrait painted. In truth my parents were more interesting than the Gethryns confined to the pages of fashionable country house living.

Like me, Anthony was an only child. As might be expected of a blue blood, he wasn't a grind and had the hackneyed grace to appear to neglect his studies. Despite the charade, he "covered himself with academic glory which outshone even that of his excellence at racquets and rugby football." Pish posh behavior—the sort of example the English aristocracy spread through innumerable novels. I'm not sure books affect readers. But if it is proved that they do, then conscientious parents of impressionable teenagers should demand that libraries ban at least a hundred and twenty years of British novels. At Oxford, Gethryn was a triple threat and became a noted historian, classicist, and mathematician. My Cambridge career was modest, indeed anonymous. Still, it was not without a tinge of color. You were, an acquaintance wrote recently, "a rather exotic figure amid the dinginess of early-60s England." Academically, Gethryn got a first, not the Gentleman's degree, a two-two like I received. Insofar as sports were concerned, I was a real gentleman. I excelled at nothing. I played water polo and rowed in several second and third college boats.

After Cambridge, I taught school. After Oxford, Anthony traveled the world for three and a half years paying his way. He had trouble deciding on a career. He was called to the bar but didn't practice. He worked for a Member of Parliament. I was admitted to law school but decided not to attend. During this time, he painted pictures and wrote novels and poetry. He earned one hundred and fifty pounds from the poetry but nothing from the novels. For my part, I published a sheaf of poems and wrote several academic books. I also wrote a biography of Tarzan who, as might be anticipated, resembled me. I also kept my hands cleaner than Gethryn's by not earning a penny. When World War I broke out, he enlisted as a private. By 1918 he was a colonel. Early in the war he spent a year in a hospital recovering from a sniper's bullet, three pieces of shrapnel, and "the newest thing in undiagnosed fevers." On his recovery, because he was fluent in German, he spent eighteen months in Berlin as a spy. After the war, his Uncle Charles died and made him financially independent. The war left him limping, indecisive, and wanting a wife. He used some of Charles's money to underwrite a weekly newspaper and eventually met an eligible widow. Her carriage made her seem tall. She had "night-black" hair, a "gracious sensibility," and a passionate mouth that also hinted at humor. As readers expected, success as an amateur detective did not elude him. Like Anthony, I limp, my right knee game, not from a wound, but from the wear of running road races. I have never spied. But I have traveled without purpose creating suspicion, making me the sort of difficult-to-taxonomize person who, because he looks nothing like a secret agent and appears (pretends) not to speak any language other than English, is often thought a spy. Unlike Gethryn I haven't solved crimes, but I have read enough mysteries to peer behind words and see things invisible to others, my similarity to the colonel being one of them. Additionally, I married a woman with dark brown hair, not quite black but a long way across the color wheel from cutesy blond. Because she did not acknowledge my similarities to Sammy, I did not mention Gethryn to Vicki.

Once upon a time I read steadily for hours. Now although reading resembles recess and is frequently a respite from work, sitting motionless eventually tires rather than invigorates. Consequently, I read in bits and pieces. In Nova Scotia I adjourned work in order to read, and adjourned reading to work. Days resembled Dagwood sandwiches. Sometimes the layers were difficult to manage, but hours themselves were sane and rarely fatiguing. Typically, I laid my book aside and split wood until my right hip throbbed. Despite two cords of wood being stored in the barn, Vicki purchased a third cord, enough to keep the stove going through the tenure of a second and perhaps third husband. The new cord lay jumbled by the entrance to the barn. I opened a folding chair and, sitting amid the loose ends of the pile, tossed wood into a wheelbarrow. Once the wheelbarrow was half-full, I rolled it into the barn and stacked the wood along a wall. Pushing the wheelbarrow as well as pushing myself out of the folding chair made my right knee ache, and I parceled the chore out among several days, and books. On the last morning, Eliza joined me. As she shoved the final load into the barn, the stack which we raised along the wall suddenly tilted and burst. The wood exploded across the floor like water cascading over a fall. Although they kicked about our feet, none of the logs hit us. "Well, darn," I said. Then we both laughed.

During breaks I did many things other than splitting wood. I pruned the golden elder and rhododendron by the barn. I hunted caterpillars scanning the upper surfaces of leaves for their frass. I wasn't successful. I fared better with black and yellow Argiopes my favorite garden spider. In the morning, dew clung to their webs transforming them into platters, pieces of silver services embellishing sight. As I searched for webs, I noticed other things: nodding ladies tresses blooming in demure white profusion, and plump mounds of blue and yellow asters, the pattern tailor-made for the pillows and sheets of a granddaughter's bed. Sometimes I stood on the porch and listened to waves sweeping across the shore and breaking on the rocks below the bluff. At low tide during calm blue mid-days I listened to silence. I forever saw things, one day a dead meadow jumping mouse, a feral cat's plaything. One afternoon I surprised a young red squirrel on the step that led from the backhouse to the pantry. The squirrel was ripping threads out of a moldy rag rug. When the squirrel noticed me, we were only two feet apart. We both froze and stared at one another. My presence didn't disturb the squirrel unduly. Almost immediately she realized I was harmless and quickly resumed tearing the rug. The squirrel would have made a good pet. If I had been a fresh country boy, I'd have tamed her and named her Molly.

Often, I didn't get beyond the pantry. Vicki brought two tubs of unsalted Virginia Diner Peanuts to Nova Scotia. Each contained two pounds and four ounces of peanuts making them difficult to hide. Atop the refrigerator were Celebration dark chocolate butter cookies. Vicki stored the cookies in a rectangular tin that once contained Oreos. Depicted on the tin was a Christmas scene. Santa Claus stood outside a house looking through a window at a little boy and girl sitting in front of a sparkling tree. In the boy's lap was a teddy bear. On his left was a low table. On it were two glasses of milk and a plate of Oreos. The girl twisted one cookie into halves. She held the chocolate half in her right hand. In her left was the vanilla half. It would soon disappear as she stared at it longingly. Inside the box was a note from my dietician, "No More Than 1 A Day Would Be Best." I changed the 1 to 4, and when Vicki scolded me for emptying the tin quickly, I said I behaved temperately and only ate two at a time, "a compromise between one and four."

The books I read initially were small. They were between-the-acts entertainments suitable for bursts of concentration but also uncomplicated and easy to put aside in order to mount a snack hunting expedition to the pantry or examine the broken cap of a boletus mushroom, the flesh of which turns blue when exposed to air. On returning to the study, I retrieved the books and began reading without caring where I left off. Among the first volumes I selected was *The Century Collegiate Handbook* published in 1926 and written by Garland Greever and Easley Jones. I didn't agree with the authors' contention that ending a sentence with a dash was "childish." Condemning "It is me" was too removed from vernacular speech to concern anyone except a fusty grammarian. When the person with my name rings a doorbell, he might be *I* or *me*, depending on my relation to the individual answering the door. I agreed that writers should avoid weighing sentences down with unrelated matters, their example being, "His face has a look of determination upon it, and he usually wears brown shoes." For formal occasions necessitating determination, the knowing always don black shoes, ideally wingtips, a matter overlooked by Greever and Jones. Clearly the authors were to the study hall, not to the manor raised. They said using *divine* to describe delights such as "Bavarian cream" was intemperate. Mother knew more about proper social grammar than the two school marms. She recognized the importance of superlatives and exaggeration and taught me the art of the compliment. "Only savages leave a dinner party" she instructed, "without singling out at least one dish and telling their hostess it was divine." The authors scorned "fine writing." How captivating my books would have been had my prose soared above pedestrian description. In the future I will dress paragraphs for The Gaudy inspired by sentences akin to those proscribed by the *Handbook*, an especially toothsome example being, "a row of pearly teeth set off to advantage the small rosebud mouth of the fair damsel." Still, Greever and Jones have educated me albeit not in the way they intended. Into every essay I will insert corking elucidations like "performed the food act at a bang-up gastronomic emporium" or following an afternoon of peanuts and crackerjacks at the ballpark describe the dinger which won the game for the home team, saying "the kid bingled a tall drive that made the horsehide ramble out into center garden."

Subjects and predicates interested me more than frontal and temporal lobes, and I didn't spend as much time on Geraldine Coster's *Psycho-Analysis for Normal People* as on the *Handbook*. Unlike Coster who noticed complexes here and there much as stargazers see constellations when they scan the night sky, I thought "Repression and Suppression" shaped manners and were the footings of courtesy and polite behavior, indeed the plinth of sanity. Moreover, I didn't believe a football game "the perfect substitute for the head-hunting forays by which the young savage proves his prowess and claims his position as a full-grown member of the tribe." However, according to Chauncey Tinker in his *Essays in Retrospect*, a volume I also read, "confessors" told Samuel Pepys that they experienced "some difficulty in persuading their penitents to abridge the tale of their sins." As astrophysicists put it, "the luminous antics that go around orbit back around." Alas, I must confess that when indulging in secondary school football, I played with both brain and teeth. When submerged under bodies and beyond the vision of referees, I occasionally nibbled on an opponent. Although too shallow to break skin, the nips so enraged adversaries that once free from the pile, they lost control and in sight of officials slugged me.

Coster often mulled sublimation, that is, doing one thing to avoid another, participating in the concrete and the seen in order to repress the unseen. I'd not be a good subject for Coster's analysis. Only after being stung by actual white-faced hornets have I yelled "shit." Never have I noticed the stings of imaginary hornets. Indeed, I don't believe they exist. Certainly they don't hang nests from branches in my rational New England. The "average man who reads a story with no object beyond the amusement of an idle hour," Coster wrote, "is not adjusting himself to reality as much as fleeing from it." Oh, dear, and the nights shall be filled with humbug, well, in a non-sublimated yard: cicadas, crickets, and katydids. Of course, some aspects of life are mysterious. Vicki and I left Storrs at four in the morning on the sixth of July and drove to Bar Harbor to catch the afternoon ferry to Yarmouth. On the previous day I got up as I habitually do at six o'clock to put the dogs outside. While I stood in the driveway watching the dogs, a bird passed overhead and seasoned the left shoulder of my pajamas. The dropping resembled whole grain mustard. Before eating breakfast, I scooped it off with a spoon and flicked it into the pachysandra by the kitchen door. I don't know whether being defecated upon was a good or bad sign. Perhaps the signification depends upon the species of bird. While two people assured me the incident indicated that I'd soon experience extraordinarily good luck, another said misfortune "deep as a pit" lay ahead.

"Time will tell," volunteered an alienist who overheard my discussing the matter in Dog Lane Café. Months have passed. Time hasn't and won't tell, and the effect produced by the bird's rude familiarity remains a mystery, not, however, one that nags my unconscious self. Not even the adept who deciphered the scratching on the Rosetta Stone could satisfactorily interpret the omens hinted at by the calligraphy of bird behavior. Every day gulls flew silently over Four Winds. Often they didn't call, but Vicki and I realized they were there. Their shadows swept across the side meadow, their wings mowing like scythes. "On the beach," a man told me, "a person can ignore the shadows of birds, but if one falls on him while he is in a field, someday he will suffer from gallstones."

From a box in the storeroom at Four Winds, I unearthed books suitable for intermittent reading. They were so boring they practically jerked me out of my armchair. Of course, boredom sometimes awakens narcoleptic readers more effectively than modafinil. Observations bright as Creeping Jenny often wind through paragraphs in the dustiest volumes. Amid the arid pages of Henry Fairfield Osborn's *Impressions of Great Naturalists* was a sentence calling John Burroughs the poet of robins and apples. Old scribblers are immune to envy, but I wish I'd had made that remark. Among other books that propelled me out of the study was *The Beauty of Wisdom* by James De Normandie. Published in 1903, the volume consisted of "Daily Readings from Some Ancient Writers for Family, School, and Private Meditation." The readings failed to inspire, and beginning with July 13, pages of the book were uncut—uncut for 119 years. I enjoyed slicing pages more than reading selections. Still, occasionally I mulled a sentence, for example, Confucius's supposedly saying "what needs no display is virtue." I copied the line after which I drifted into a snake oil mood and wrote, "people should see real, not television virtue." I took notes in the delusion that the phrases would stretch weedy and rank through the platitudinous topiary of "good news" palaver. They didn't. Frequently the phrases I jotted down prompted idiosyncratic associations. On Alvin Howard Sanders calling overly bred lap dogs "canine canaries" in *The Road to Dumbiedykes*, Vicki's and my three small rescue mutts came to mind. "They are our 'Outside House Sparrows,'" I thought.

In July a hermit thrush sang from the top of a dead spruce at dawn and at dusk. When I heard the song, I stopped what I was doing and listened. The music was a bridge across time into the soft bank of other summers. Thirty years ago, eiderdowns of moths covered the screen doors at night. Butterflies flew dappled above the blueberry field, and like Maggie and her gray lover, Vicki and I were young. The children were our green grove and daisies, blossoming and unceremoniously loving. In something of the same way passages from books were bridges, not to the past, however, but to gravelly contemplation. In *A Promise of Ankles*, Alexander McCall Smith stated, "we must keep alive the happiness we experience before the world closes in on us." Yes, I thought, but we must also embrace, maybe treasure, sadness and grief, the senses of loss and of time's passing, loneliness, and muffled anxiety. A person should do so that when he is alive, his drying bones live, so that the song of a hermit thrush guides him into nowhere and everywhere.

Occasionally I abandoned a volume of intermittent reading because its tediousness so mesmerized me that I was liable to spend unhealthy, backside-expanding hours in the study. Even worse, afterward I'd have carried the reading into the kitchen and spoiled a week of conversations at the dinner table. The most seductive of such books was *Ask me another! The Question Book*, a compilation of "Forty Information Tests" with two thousand questions and answers. For each correct answer a reader received two points. Usually, two people competed against each other although a few people measured themselves against imaginary opponents. In one of the "general" quizzes, the Yale English professor William Lyon Phelps amassed 92 points defeating Robert Benchley by eight points. In the "special" sports quiz, Grantland Rice made a perfect score. The quizzes exposed holes that age opened in my memory. No longer did I know Frans Hals painted "The Laughing Cavalier." At dinner during the single evening I tested quizzes, labeling them "intellectual hors d'oeuvres," I succeeded in naming three of the Seven Wonders of the Ancient World, knocking off the Pyramids, the Hanging Gardens of Babylon and the Colossus at Rhodes. For the record Eliza matched me and went one better, mentioning the Lighthouse at Alexandria. Only Vicki recognized that "Keep that schoolgirl complexion" was the slogan of Palmolive soap. No one associated "Eventually, why not now?" with Gold Medal Flour, but Edward knew that "when the Assyrian came down like a wolf on the fold" his cohorts were gleaming in purple and gold. Francis was in Connecticut when I proctored that first and last exam. I intended to save the "Special" science test for him, but Vicki said the barrage of questions during the meal was less interesting than spinning the lazy Susan like a roulette wheel and guessing where it would stop.

Thoreau said reading "true books" was a "noble exercise." Using novel-reading as an exemplar of an ignoble pursuit, he wrote that the result of reading slight volumes led to "dullness of sight, a stagnation of the vital circulations, and a general deliquium and sloughing off of all the intellectual faculties." At eighty, people don't read to shape character. They don't think young people have important advice to give to the old, except instructions on operating mechanical conveniences supposed to simplify but which often complicate. Neither do they classify books as true and untrue. Their reactions are more verbal than intellectual, and they mutter things like "not worth a damn" or "a humdinger—not to be missed." Certainly, during the summer, I laid books aside that did not appeal to me. However, I didn't consider whether they were noble or true. Such concerns indigest students in tenth grade English classes. On Eliza's suggestion I opened John Scalzi's *Redshirts*. I shut it after learning that, for starters, Borgovian Land Worms ate a man's face before gobbling down the rest of him. Later Eliza told me that appreciation of the novel depended upon knowledge of *Star Trek*. I grew up before television became addictive. The fiction I like is earthy and earthbound, and I have never watched *Star Trek*.

To ease my landing after bailing out of *Redshirts*, I reread George Garrett's *Whistling in the Dark*. George gave me the book in 1992. As I read, I wondered if anyone anywhere was rereading a book I wrote thirty years ago. George's world was familiar. Among his subjects were sports, Sewanee, and Princeton. Two of his coaches had one eye. For my part I knew three one-eyed poets. Like George, I played games, rather toyed at them. They taught me I'd never excel at anything, a wonderfully freeing lesson. George's landscape was anecdotal and rich with vaudeville tales plucked from and honed by years of teaching. Although I have long been stitched hidebound into discipline, my learning and reading, indeed living, have paradoxically been harum-scarum affairs. Matters that might have driven Coster's nervous subjects to the Chuckle House only made me chuckle. Thoreau's sacerdotal prose quotes well, but his evangelism is limited. Off the page simple matters become complex. The straightforward often proves crooked, and the crooked, straightforward. Instead of instilling confidence, knowledge can undermine assurance while arrogance and ignorance foster it. "Accuracy is plastic," a literary woman said to me; "eventually it becomes brittle." Maybe, but sometimes it limbers like neatsfoot oil. During a walk along the beach at Salmon River, Vicki counted 129 buoys attached to a breakwater. To be accurate, she counted three times, and her brother Geoff, once. "Write the figure down," Vicki said. "Put it in a book. Many readers are counters. For such people counting leads to the unaccountable. Numbers fill silences and arouse their imaginations. They can so burnish people's lives that they whistle through the dark." "What?" I said lifting a notebook out of the pocket of my shorts.

On the page, unlike daily life, asides can be thrust aside effortlessly. Surprises, though, clutter life and happy books. In *Whistling in the Dark*, I found two scraps of paper, both homemade bookmarks. The first was half a page I'd ripped out of a "Reporter's Notebook." On it appeared the names of two stores I noticed in Port of Spain four years ago, "Cow Heel Soup Shop" next door to "Johnny Pet Store." I copied the names because I imagined the shop's expanding its menu to include stews, the main ingredients coming from Johnny, all rich and green in hot tureens, as Lewis Carroll put it, mock hamster, and goldfish who lost their ways without the guidance of a porpoise. I quickly realized that the concept was fey, not worth a paragraph, and I jettisoned it soon after recording the names of the stores. On the second bookmark was a joke written in an unfamiliar hand and sent to me, or perhaps to someone else, by a forgotten acquaintance. Two American tourists entered a bar outside the Vatican in Rome. After having been there a while, they noticed an elderly man sitting in a dark corner swilling wine. "Do you know who that is?" the first tourist said. "It's the Pope." "No," the second tourist responded. "The Pope wouldn't be alone in here. He'd have a couple of his Cardinals buddies with him." "Huh," the first tourist said. "Let's ask him." "Excuse me, sir, for intruding," the tourist began, "but we were wondering if you might be." Before the tourist finished his sentence, the old man slammed his glass down on the table spilling his wine and shouted, "Go to Hell and mind your own goddamn business, you inquisitive bastards." "What a shame," the second tourist said as he and his friend walked away from the man. "He didn't answer the question, and now we will never know if he is the Pope."

5

The Pond is Dry. Part II

I read in Vicki's and my bedroom as well as in the study. The bedroom was on the second floor, and my arthritic knee and the debilitating medicines I took made ascending and descending the stairs arduous. I crabbed my way up, placing my right hand flat on the step above me, my left a flange locked on the railing. I climbed and descended a step at a time thumping peg-legged, placing my left foot atop the step above me then following with the right. Once both feet were on the same step, I raised my left foot again and placed it on the next step. Although I came down in the same fashion, often the descent was more difficult. Jack and Suzie were old. Instead of their being my companions, I was their nurse and protector. They slept and napped upstairs. They were unsteady on their legs, and often I cradled one of them in my free arm while I climbed or descended the stairs. For my part I fretted about falling. In June six years ago a stone wall collapsed while I stood atop it studying pheasants. My left thigh slammed down on a rounded loaf-shaped granite rock. During the remainder of the summer I limped, and colors wheeled through my thigh—sooty black, purple, yellow, and brown. At dawn one morning, three years ago at Four Winds my leg buckled as I raced down the stairs pursuing Mee, our third rescue dog. I hurried carelessly because I thought she was about to have an accident in the downstairs hall. Early this summer I tripped over a fallen spruce at the edge of a boggy wood and fell into a trap of broken limbs, bracken and cinnamon ferns high as my shoulders. Although I walked with two ski poles to brace myself, I had trouble getting up and kept tumbling over. When I eventually got on my feet, I was so splotched with red that someone unaware of my penchant for unexpected descents might have thought I had been robbing a strawberry patch.

Because I worried about falling, once upstairs I remained there longer than I did in the study. Consequently, I read more pages at a sitting. However, the dogs had aged into incontinence, and when they approached me, I took them downstairs and into the meadow by the porch. I also took them outside at 11:30 at night and 5:00 in the morning. I woke myself automatically. On returning to the bedroom, I read until 6:00 when I again went downstairs for early chores. I slipped Wellingtons over my pajama legs, cleaned ashes out of the stove, then took them and the slop bowl next to the sink outside and dumped them in a grove of dead spruce. Unless spider webs distracted me, I turned around and immediately walked back to the porch. I laid the bowl and ash pan down and picking up a trowel roamed the meadow searching for dog droppings. Sometimes I crisscrossed the meadow methodically. Other times I rolled about like a loose ball of yarn. I imagined hunting pirate treasure. Once I discovered booty, I tossed it into bay or under a hedge of meadow sweet. I found an astonishing number of pieces of eight. Occasionally, I bragged about my piratical eye to Vicki and informed her about the loot. She was never interested. Once back in the kitchen I lined the slop bowl with wax paper and laid a fire in the stove. On the bottom I crumpled newsprint, mostly from a stack of papers I picked up in

1988. On the print I laid kindling, usually fragments of old shingles. These I topped off with matchwood that I split in the barn. Once the fire blazed, I tossed in good sized firewood, not too large, however, because several years ago after the big kitchen stove died, we replaced it with a smaller, summer-house priced one that had belonged to a widow who cooked modest meals.

Lastly, I took off my Wellingtons, placed them beneath a shelf in the small pantry, put on my slippers, brewed a pot of tea, and ate breakfast. I always had granola or shredded wheat, a banana, and berries, these last blueberries and raspberries usually picked by Vicki and with Eliza's help when she was present. Blackberries were scarce, but in September I picked enough for a week's breakfasts, in the process mincing my arms and hands. While eating I ruminated. I can count backward from a hundred to one as fast as I can count forward from one to a hundred. Yet, I cannot do the same with the alphabet. I start quickly with Z, Y, X, and W, but I invariably stumble and collapse around P or O. The failure puzzles me because I've spent decades writing books and bedding down with words and letters, not numbers.

By the time I finished breakfast, other people began to appear, and the dogs had made their rickety ways down the steps and were asleep in their "lower boudoir," three little oval beds, two near the kitchen table and one under a buffet, the top of this last a jumble of keys, wallets, glasses, pads and pencils for lists, all the cluttering paraphernalia needed for a drive to Yarmouth or to Salmon River. Immediately after breakfast I went back upstairs, took off my pajamas, and put on day clothes, after which I busied myself in the study trying to think and appreciate. On some luminous mornings I walked down the lane to the bluff overlooking the Gulf of Maine. A bald eagle summered in a wedge of spruce. I spotted him occasionally, and the sight always excited me. However, few fish now washed ashore, and the beach was usually so bare it looked like a desert. Consequently, I suspected the eagle fed on Jonah crabs who half-buried themselves in the sand. On both sides of the lane, insect and animal life had also diminished. At times the landscape seemed a green board at the front of a lecture hall, its surface scrubbed bare before classes began. As I limped along, I scanned the fields and woods bordering the lane in hopes of glimpsing the life that decades ago flourished in gay profusion. "Man is the great destroyer," Vicki said. "He specializes in pesticides and ugliness. We are ruining the planet for our species." "All things bright and beautiful, / All creatures great and small, / All things wise and wonderful, / Dioxin, glyphosate, and pyrethroids killed them all," I muttered.

I couldn't kennel the black dog of melancholy, but during my morning ambles I noticed enough small things to make me feel less forlorn. One day a white admiral butterfly trailed me down the lane, flicking his wings and puddling, winking, maybe laughing, at me. Not until later did I recall the clouds of butterflies I saw decades ago, "prisms of joy," Edward called them. I lifted a woolly bear caterpillar across a puddle. He was dressed formally. A yellow cummerbund bound his middle, and I assumed he did not want water to stain his appearance. Was he grateful? Do actions really speak louder than words? He didn't thank me, but once amid dry grass, he uncurled and contentedly bundled away. I have long read poetry not to see life steadily and whole but as it might be, to color a mood and to drape illusion over the actual. As I walked back toward the house, "April Rain," a saccharine poem by Robert Loveman came to mind. Too slight for seriousness, the verse is a sweetener, artificial, but momentarily appealing especially when a person is alone, mulling, and disgruntled.

> "It isn't raining rain to me, / It's raining daffodils; / In every dimpled drop I see / Wild flowers on the hills; / The clouds of gray engulf the day; / And overwhelm the town; / It isn't raining rain to me, / It's raining roses down."

Another day a black-capped chickadee landed on a twig four feet from my arm. She looked at me then hopped closer and cocking her head studied my hand as if begging a treat. Like my reading, pleasures of the walks were intermittent. Many creatures I remembered were not present, among them, yellow warblers spinning through the brush, mosquitos sounding like dental air scalers, and then grey deerflies so bedeviling that I ran to escape them. Once upon a good fairy time, mourning cloak caterpillars fattened in the willow beside the side meadow. Clusters left the tree together, and breasting seas of grass, hung cocoons on the house and backhouse. Parasitic wasps preyed upon the cocoons, but many caterpillars pupated successfully, and while their wings unfolded and dried, they dangled from the clapboard like Christmas decorations. The willow itself was now dying, and several afternoons I removed dead limbs from the tree. I hadn't thought about the caterpillars for years, but this summer two pupated successfully on the barn. "Ornaments for an Advent Calendar," I said. I wanted life to return and again adorn the holy days of summer. People often see what they envision. For the first time in many summers, I watched gray cross spiders weaving webs across our windows at night. They didn't trap large or modest sized insects. They caught tiny white grass moths. The moths looked like splinters broken from splinters, but they were food enough for the spiders, and me.

At the conclusion of *Walden*, Thoreau told an instructive anecdote. An insect laid an egg in an apple tree. Later the apple tree became a table. Eventually the egg hatched, and more than sixty years after being deposited in the wood, a "strong and beautiful bug" bored out of a leaf of the table. Who knows what "winged life, whose egg has been buried for ages under many concentric layers of woodenness in the dead dry life of society," Thoreau said, "may unexpectedly come forth from amidst society's most trivial and handselled furniture, to enjoy its perfect summer life." Dreaming comes easier to the inert than it does to active people who experience and as a result know. Prolific writers realize that paragraphs won't burst from their dead books winged and acclaimed.

One afternoon I picked a dragonfly off the barn floor. Clumps of dusty spiderwebs clogged the insect's wings preventing it from flying. When I placed the dragonfly on my shirt, it dug its tarsi into the cloth. While it clung to me, I stripped the adhesive threads off its wings rolling them into tiny balls. Afterward I inserted an index finger under the dragonfly and pried it free from my shirt. It perched on my finger for a moment then shaking its wings, it fell into flight and soared out of sight. Not only do I sometimes imagine the creatures I rescue will enjoy lovely, winged lives, but that as a result I'll reap beautiful moments. Maybe like the blue bird of happiness, a dragonfly will perch on my shoulder and raise my spirits. Saving the dragonfly made me think well of myself and the thought was good enough. Moreover, good deeds are simply deeds. If asked, other dragonflies would surely have urged me to ignore the plight of their fellow Anisoptera. The dragonfly I rescued was a dragonhunter, a cannibal who feeds on her flying relatives.

Taking the dogs outside near midnight wasn't a chore. Some nights I woke myself at three o'clock, and leaving the house, stood in the side yard. Formerly I knew the constellations and read the sky. This year, days were crowded and wordy, and I did not want to diagram the beautiful immensity that arched overhead and cupped the horizons. I never missed full moons. I went outside early in the evening to see them rise gold and yellow then returned later when they spilled silver light across the fields. Only twice did I hear great horned owls calling. On both occasions they called at full moon, the first time at Buck Moon, the second at Harvest or Full Corn Moon. This summer the night sky wasn't an anthology packed with myth and stories about improbable heroes and lovers. Instead, it brought poetry to mind, not lyrics exploding in symbols like meteors but uplifting lines that encouraged quiet thought. No matter how my vision scanned the stars, my feet remained grounded in "The Green Grassy Way." "Lead, Kindly Light," I whispered silently quoting Newman, "The night is dark, and I am far from home—/ Lead thou me on!" A younger person wouldn't have recited those lines, neither would Thoreau's "children of Aurora" nor the exuberant classroom me dispensing optimism like soda pop. Perhaps to balance the tone of Newman's yearning, I also quoted lighter, light-bringing verse from Sarah Williams's "The Old Astronomer to His Pupil." "Though my soul may set in darkness, / It will rise in perfect light. / I have loved the stars too fondly / To be fearful of the night."

Vicki's and my bedroom was a dormer. Built over the kitchen and pantry, it was twice the size of the other bedrooms in the house. In the middle of the room a brick chimney ran up from the pantry through the floor and out the ceiling. In front of it sat a nineteenth century iron stove. The stove had been connected to the chimney but had been detached when the chimney was lined and rebuilt. The stove now served as a small table across which a team of metal oxen rescued from an antique store pulled a cart loaded with wood. Along three sides of the room windows opened facing the north, south, and the west. From all three the Gulf of Maine was visible, sweeping into Beaver River and curling around to the breakwater in Port Maitland in the south and to the north stretching, flexing, until it disappeared behind the dark barrier of Black Point a mile away. On muggy mornings mist covered our fields. Sometimes it resembled a shroud, others, a soft swaddling cream. In the evening beyond the west windows, the sun set amid rays, throws of color, and frequently jeweled ladders, their steps climbing across the water then disappearing under the horizon. Vicki's bed sagged in the middle, and she dubbed it "The Bucket," often singing a shanty when she got into the bed, "hearty, hearty, ho, off to sea in a bucket I go." My bed sloped precariously to the left. No matter where I began the night, by morning I was clinging to the side of the mattress. Moreover, the bed moved mysteriously toward the middle of the room, and well before I fell asleep my pillow slipped between the head of the bed and the wall. Retrieving the pillow was difficult. Once under the bed it behaved like a limpet and clung to the floor, causing land-lubbering me to bark like a sea dog.

Nevertheless, despite the bed's tendency to keel over, I read many books upstairs. A number were heftier than those I perused in the study. Initially I believed I chose thicker volumes because I intended to avoid traipsing up and down the stairs and popping in and out of the house. I expected to be comparatively sedentary and to concentrate longer. I was wrong. After retirement, distractions are us. They occupy minds and appoint vacant hours. The books were a happenstance collection. Perhaps a broth of volumes describes them better, among the ingredients, Van Wyck Mason's romances, Trollope's Manor House novels, Philip Kerr's historical mystery *Dark Matter*, Alexander McCall Smith's accounts of Ulf Varg, a quirky Swedish detective in charge of investigating sensitive crimes, and then my favorite, Nina Fedorova's *The Family* published in 1940 and describing the frangible lives led by the Russian owners and the peripatetic inhabitants of a boarding house in the British Concession of Tientsin, China in the late 1930s. In truth, reading upstairs was as intermittent as reading downstairs. The difference was that when I laid a book aside, I remained in the bedroom. My wanderings were mental not physical, and I easily shifted my attention from Kerr's Tower of London in the seventeenth century to Mason's Savannah in 1779 during the Revolutionary War.

Usually, though, I didn't immediately open another book. Often people don't see what they notice every day. To Thoreau the bedroom would have resembled a stall in the "Augean stables." It wasn't filled with "acres of land." But it reflected years of tilling and mowing and contained items not gathered during "a fool's life," but simply, and unconsciously, collected during ordinary days, little things that lightened the loads that Thoreau said crushed and smothered. Certainly, everything in the room, including myself, was corruptible and ultimately destined to fall prey to "moth and rust." But so what, so damn what? Age teaches that "Fragility, thy name is life." When I broke from reading and glanced around me, what I saw intrigued and pleased me as much as, or maybe more than signatures of well-wrought earnest paragraphs. Thoreau wrote captivating prose, but he didn't appreciate the magic of things. Such magic is personal and evanescent, but it can transform. At times while looking about the room, I forgot books.

On Vicki's bed lay six cloth sleep-awake dolls: Dorothy, Dolores, Diedre, Amanda, Abigail, and Arabella, the last three vacationing on Eliza's bed when she was at Four Winds. The dolls were ten inches tall and with their arms spread eight inches wide. On one side they were awake; on the other, asleep. Their hair was yarn, Amanda's blond, Abigail's red, and Arabella's white. The hair stuck out from each side of their heads in pigtails and was held in place by ribbons. Their eyes looked like little moons, and each eyebrow had three lashes. These pointed up when the dolls were awake and hung down when they were asleep. Vicki had been the dolls' mother since she was a little girl sixty-five years ago, something I hadn't thought about before. Indeed, I don't think I ever looked at the dolls until this summer. The sight made me sigh with affection. Thoreau said "an infinite expectation of the dawn" should keep people awake. Thoreau did not live long enough to know that dawns ebb, and one is left with glimpses of the past that was and is, the past that could have been, and the past that will never be.

On a table stood two hand-carved wooden figures, each nine inches tall. While one of the figures held an ax in his right hand and was a woodsman, the other was a fisherman, in his left hand a rod and slung over his shoulder a large fish, probably a trout. Trailing the two men across the table were four wooden pigs, three hogs and a piglet. In a way the room was a barnyard for small versions of big animals. A pair of Belgian work horses dragged logs. A primitive tailless ox pulled a cart. Whenever I looked away from a book, I noticed things: five paintings, one acrylic and new depicting a farmhouse atop a drumlin overlooking an eroded beach, the others old and oil, three of these of breaking waves. The last portrayed the rugged landscape around and above a mountain lake, The scene looked influenced by Albert Bierstadt's western art, say, a canvas like "Among the Sierra Nevada Mountains." A decade ago Vicki discovered the painting in a warehouse. She paid fifteen dollars for it and gave it to me on my birthday. Vicki and I had purchased only a few of the items in the room: two prints, one of lupin, the other of a Mansard house that twenty years ago perched precariously on a tongue of rock at Cape St. Mary. Storms beat the house into abandonment. However, sunsets restored its youth, and until it was demolished, in the afternoon the house blushed like a young girl. We also bought two bubble glass plates. In one, three blue angel fish swiveled through a broom of kelp. In the other, a dragonfly settled on the flowerhead of a cattail. Spread wide to absorb warmth, the dragonfly's wings were clear but speckled with blue and hints of yellow which shivered into awareness only when lights were on. Most things in the room were older than the books I read: a leather hatbox with a concave top, a framed bouquet of daisies and roses fashioned from colored tinfoil, probably by a farm wife during a cold winter near the end of the nineteenth century, and then wooden models of three ships, all three-masted barques, one in a bottle.

The furniture was too old to harbor beautiful bugs. Against the wall to the left of my bed was a sugar chest. Crammed in it was so much clothing that the lid had sprung. I don't know to whom the clothes belonged. I only opened the chest to hide and retrieve passports and cash. My own clothes were in an ancient chest of drawers. The drawers were so stuffed with clothes that opening them was difficult. Each summer I urged Vicki not to pack additional clothes for me. She did not listen, and every July I crammed more clothes into the chest. My days of elegance have passed. I like the crumpled familiarity of ratty dress. My suit wearing days are over. Those that have not furnished banquets for moths, Vicki has donated to Good Will. Like a sensible octogenarian, I have grown accustomed to, and liked the rumpled *Me*. Because Four Winds lacked a shower and the tub stood high off the floor on clawed feet, every day I was slightly soiled. Getting in and out of the tub was so hard that during the first thirty-seven days in Nova Scotia, I took only six partial baths, that is, some scrubbing every 6.1 days. A Thoreauvian might assume I'd heeded the call for simplicity. No, I responded to exigency that, as a person ages, evolves into necessity. This change affects writing. I have abandoned complex sentences. Let youth who does not understand and believes it should understand embrace complexity. Short declarative sentences suit their elders.

Against the chimney was a wooden seaman's chest. Three feet long and sixteen inches high and wide, it was too heavy for me, and, probably, for choppy seas to shift. Spots pooled and blotched the lid, and stains rippled over it like ridges of sand on a rough shoreline. Vicki called the chest "an ugly old thing," and if it had not been weighty would have buried it in the storeroom. During their lives, old people generally sail through a few storms. Before they are deep-sixed ashore permanently, lesions and scales, warts, moles, and keratoses black, brown, and tan splotch them. As a result, ugly things no longer are unappealing. But Vicki is eleven years younger than I, and her aesthetic sense differs from mine. The chest wasn't lovely, but because it was discolored it intrigued me, and I wondered what seas it had ridden. Had it "flown" on a clipper ship to San Francisco, the boat's sails billowed by gold rush fever? How many times had it rounded Cape Horn and followed an albatross through Drake Passage? Had its owner smoked opium and loaded silk and tea in China? Eventually my imagination returned to the bedroom and dry dock. Then I put the chest to utilitarian use and on the lid stacked the volumes I considered reading.

One of the first books I read upstairs was Frank Parker Day's *The Autobiography of a Fisherman*. I found it in a box amid a stack of Latin textbooks. The volume wasn't substantial. I'm not a fisherman, but I read the book because it was inscribed to Vicki's grandmother. "For my beloved Margaret with precious memories of our Lake Annis summer together," Paul wrote on Maundy Thursday, 1931. Vicki's grandmother was a widow and spent summers near Beaver River at an artist's colony on Lake Annis. In residence at the same time were Day and his wife Mabel, a painter. Day had led an active life. He was a Rhodes scholar, an athlete who won a blue at Oxford, a writer, an academic, and a distinguished officer during World War I. He and his wife lived in a cabin on Lake Annis. Living was cheap, and treatment for a blow Day received in the back during the war had depleted their savings. Like that of many scribblers, Day's life was more interesting than his book. Day strung the major events of his years together like buoys on a fishing line. "Knowing too much," a character in James Hilton's *Random Harvest* said, "stamps one as a bit of an outsider." Hilton got it slightly wrong. Knowing too much about a subject and informing others makes a person tedious. He drives auditors away thereby making himself an outsider. Day fished through two hundred pages. In Nova Scotia fishing is a literal and literary activity, but if the inscription had not made me curious, I would have thrown the hook after fifty pages. In most books, a few statements engage me. College, Day declared, was worthwhile "if only for my introduction to Wordsworth." In Wordsworth's nature poetry, Day testified, "I found many of the things I had already felt. Literature pleases us when we find in it an expression of our inarticulate selves." The same was true of me. I wasn't a fisherman, but I was a catcher, a gentle boy who never bruised, much less cooked and ate his catches.

On the chest, books didn't sink under an easy chair lost to sight and mind. Rather they slipped into groups of similar topics. *Lost River, The Waters of Remembrance* was a memoir. In it, Harry Thurston described the streams in which he went "a-fishing in." Thurston is from Yarmouth and is a fine naturalist. Not long before writing *Lost River*, he suffered a near-fatal fall and two bouts of prostate cancer. The tone of the volume was elegiac, and along with fish Thurston hooked and retrieved memories, these last the piscine equivalents of my baiting days with books. The actual lost river was the Annis, not a surprise because I now anticipate discovering familiar things or an expression of my inarticulate self in much of my reading. If I don't perceive ties, I frequently claim to have found them. In *Psycho-Analysis*, Coster cited an often-quoted line from a play popular at the end of the nineteenth century. "It is better to lie a little than to be unhappy much." Yes, and on the page, lies are effective conjunctions. In any case Thurston speculated that rivers reminded people of themselves and their "own wandering passage through space and time." "Ever changing" and subject to "temperamental highs and lows, they are nevertheless always there—even when we do not see them or fish them. They are not abstractions." In Connecticut during summers, the Fenton River sometimes contracts into puddles scattered along a dry bed like liver-spots on the backs of an aged man's hands. But like all metaphors, Thurston's hypothesis was as inaccurate as accurate, as momentarily satisfying as dissatisfying. For the record I don't remember experiencing highs and lows. I've simply flowed, my water level neither rising nor falling. Rather than moody, I am placid. Moreover, although calm of mind can stifle passion and put acquaintances to sleep, it is a major ingredient of happiness.

Water ran through many of my upstairs volumes. The location of Four Winds influenced my selections. Henry de Vere Stacpoole's *The Gates of Morning* was a Pacific Island romance, its sets cluttered with palm trees, canoes, lagoons, egregious violence, misplaced and displaced people, wayfaring scoundrels, and mystical gobbledygook. Much to the pleasure of the literary anarchist lurking inside me, Stacpoole lost control of the wheel of plot and becoming a narrative assassin bumped off his characters. They all died after catching measles infesting a Dead Ship. After locking *The Gates*, I continued sailing the South Seas and boarded Melville's *Omoo.* The Gulf of Maine is too cold for swimming. In contrast, a reader can paddle comfortably in the South Seas for a volume or two. "Omoo" means rover or island wanderer, and in the novel Omoo roamed Polynesia meandering from village to village. His experiences rarely startled, and suffering from a dose of Stacpoole flu, I longed for a gaggle of Ambrose Bierce's cannibals to run their outriggers into the story and end the novel and its hero. For the record, Bierce's epicures were gastronomes of "the old school" who preserved the simpler tastes and adhered "to the natural diet of the pre-pork period."

When a reader explores an exotic land, he will likely stumble across memorable descriptions. Omoo's shipmate Rope Yard was a forlorn, stunted, hook-visaged mortal, "one of those, whom you know at a glance to have been tried hard and long in the furnace of affliction." When his friends haul a Polynesian youth to an eminent tattooer, "it behooves the professor to have a nice eye, for a suit to be worn for life should be well cut." The quality of flesh also matters, although Melville does not mention it. Today most tattooers practice on such cheap materials that the dyes run and the original patterns, be they herringbone, houndstooth, or pinstripe, meld into green and blue after-dinner stains. At the conclusion of the book, Omoo bids good-bye to his companion Doctor Long Ghost. After shaking the doctor heartily by the hand, he says that he had "never seen or heard of him since," not unlike a reader's closing a novel knowing he won't reread it. Afterward, Omoo's ship sails. By noon Tahiti "had gone down in the horizon; and all before us," Omoo states, "was the wide Pacific."

The final sentence was romantic with possibility. An oldster would only mouth it wistfully. Nowadays when I embark in a book, I realize the horizon is near. I'm not boarding an airplane and telling family I "don't know when I'll be back again." Still after I unmoor from actuality and roll forward in an easy chair, the immediate recedes for a while. Intermittently between constructing his cabin and hoeing beans, Thoreau read "one or two shallow books of travel." He read them until "that employment," more accurately the absence of employment, caused him to be ashamed of himself. "In all men," Henry Ware Smith wrote, "in some degree the wilderness wish exists, however hidden in the haste and habit of the world we make." Most old men have experienced clipper ship moments in which they journeyed beyond Convention and Expectation and hovered near "Good Hope."

Clipper ships often docked at Melbourne. I docked for two and a half years at Perth. Richard Halliburton was a boyhood companion, and since childhood guided by travel writers, I've traipsed innumerable wildernesses. This summer I read two travel books: Carl Hoffman's *The Lunatic Express* and Nick Hunt's *Walking the Woods and the Water*. For 159 days Hoffman circled the globe traveling on the world's most dangerous buses, trains, boats, and planes through and across forbidding and forbidden landscapes. "I'd taken the train from Bamako not just because it was so famously bad, but because it brought me to Dakar, from which a ship named *MV Le Joola* had sailed six years before—and sunk in the second worst maritime disaster in history." Of the 1863 confirmed passengers, only 60 survived, one of whom was a woman. For his part Hunt spent 221 days walking 2500 miles across Europe retracing, and by necessity and choice occasionally deviating from the walk Patrick Leigh Fermor began in 1933. Fermor's walk is a touchstone of contemporary travel. Described in three books, it is an icon to which adventure travelers genuflect. Hoffman's and Hunt's volumes startled and entertained me. Occasionally their footsteps crossed a path I'd forgotten, and recollection made me glance away from a page, not regretful for experiences unlived but thankful I'd escaped the temptations of disruptive possibility. Age insulated me from armchair envy, and the aftertaste of the books differed greatly from that I'd have enjoyed had I been young. Downstairs my family bustled noisily about. Unlike Omoo I never jumped ship and shed responsibility. In the past I celebrated "free spirits." Such praise now seems "folio admiration"—not motivated by belief, but because the arrangements of nouns, verbs, and thoughts worked well on the page. Hunt's and Hoffman's wanderings did not evoke awe as once they might have done. They struck me as absurd and resembled the literary swings and slides writers left behind after they matured. My attitude resembled that of Thoreau more than I admitted. How much better and perhaps more difficult to describe the ordinary and the colorless. "That's an apologia for your books," Vicki said. She was correct, but I was comfortable and too domesticated to behave like a circus animal and jump from one ring into another. "My thoughts and doings are too flat for hormonal readers," I replied. "But they are mete for the old." Later, after stretching my legs which had gone to sleep and become heavy while I read, I mused, "what Time has given me, it will give to all people who walk 'the woods and the water,' if they are fortunate."

Books furnished the study and the bedroom, but I spent as much time outside as I did inside. In the past I humped across fields and stumbled and sagged through wetlands. Now I ambled. In previous summers when an obstacle blocked me in the woods, I twisted and bent until I found a way around it. Now I reversed direction. I didn't climb rocky slopes or vault over stone walls. Neither did I shimmy down foundation holes or hoist myself over fallen trees. I carried walking sticks to steady myself in case the ground tipped. Instead of blazing through brambles kicking their foothold runners aside, I walked in tracks dug by skidders. When tired, I leaned against trees wrapping my arms around limbs and trunks. I didn't sit because I couldn't get back on my feet without rolling onto my stomach, digging the toes of my boots into the dirt, and grabbing hunks of ground with my hands, push up with my fists. From the point of view of the vanished younger me, I was preternaturally cautious. I stayed near the house and rarely ventured alone beyond hailing distance. The person I was forty years ago would have smiled paternally and thought my temerity unjustified, if not slightly nuts. Thoreau got it wrong. The old have a great deal to teach the young; the young are just not mature enough to learn.

I accompanied family on strolls to Black Point and along the beaches at Salmon River and Cape St. Mary. Family members shortened their natural strides and tempered the ebullience that tempted them to race along the shore. Nonetheless, I lagged. The lower back of Jack, our fifteen-year-old dog, sagged and his legs wobbled. At the start of walks Jack accompanied me, but eventually the sunlight pepped him up. His legs steadied, and he trotted ahead, although he returned periodically to ensure I was all right. Thoreau said people needed "the tonic of wildness." At eighty, walking alone suited me. If I had been surrounded by family, the walks would have been enjoyable, and affectionate, but they would have been communal, not personal. As years alter reading, so time changes a person's interests, if only for a moment. Often this summer I needed the tonic of loneliness. Like Thoreau's wildness, it sharpened sight and appreciation. Temporarily I forgot the diminution of insect and animal life. Melancholy dissolved as I looked at flowers. In describing the recurring fortunes of his relatives, Thurston wrote that repetition was "a reassurance that all is well in one's life—that rhythms may repeat, patterns hold." The flowers I saw were familiar, the companions of my budding and blooming and now wilting. If heaven were an actual place, not the pinched creation of the covetous, its streets would be paved with flowers, not gold. Neither would the walls of the New Jerusalem be jasper. In early summer they'd be Queen Anne's lace and garnished "with all manner" of precious flowers, forget-me-nots, pasture roses, sow thistles, germander, purple orchis, beach pea, vetch, yellow cow lily, pickerel weed, and lady's slippers. After Queen Anne's lace withered, flat-topped asters would replace it. And to Hell, literally to Hell, with the wall's sapphire, chalcedony, emerald, beryl, and amethyst. In their places, fall dandelions, clumps of Queen of the Meadow white and cooling as snow, Gerardia, its blooming so short-lived, the blossoms seem almost stillborn, but purple and royal, indeed sanctified, evening primrose, mallow, and jewelweed, hummingbirds hovering around this last like thirsty souls. The city itself would not be "pure gold, like unto clear glass." No, the city would be bright with wild raisin and winterberry, spruce hung with old man's beard, mountain ash, alder its dark cones rattling like tambourines, and, here and there, mushrooms: toy-like puffballs, fly agaric, orange and blood red, and destroying angel, white as a cumulus cloud, neither of these last two poisonous, enchanting but not poisonous.

We arrived in Nova Scotia with three dogs. We left with two. Sixteen years ago, Vicki rescued Suzie from the pound in East Hartford. When the dogcatcher caught her, Suzie was living on the street. She weighed ten pounds and was a blend of Chihuahua and mystery mongrel. I thought her handsome. She was black with brown streaks on her muzzle giving her a barbered appearance. With long, thin legs, she ran fast and endlessly and accompanied Vicki and me on our meanderings in Storrs. In Nova Scotia, the beach was her racetrack. Not until the last year of her life, when her sight and hearing deteriorated and she suffered from canine dementia causing her sense of direction to spin like a broken magnetic needle on a compass, did we leash her. Initially Vicki chose her because when she walked past the dogs at the pound, Suzie stood at the door of her cage and stared. "Not barking," Vicki recalled, "not even moving, as if she knew, as silly as this sounds, I'd select her." Although she stayed close to us in the house and out, Suzie was not overly affectionate and didn't hang on our heels, jump on our legs, and become an underfoot nuisance. When I returned from class or Vicki from the grocery, she wagged her tail with happy abandon, but she never licked us and didn't like being held. Somehow, she became my girl and occasionally when I sat on the battered couch in the television room, I lifted her up and she snuggled against my thigh while I rubbed her ears and neck. The contentment generated by the rubbing probably affected me more than Suzie. While I rubbed, simple care vanished. During her final months when life puzzled her, I rubbed her often hoping that touch would reassure her. I also stroked her to reassure myself and lessen the ache I felt seeing her decline. I am a sentimentalist. Sentiment often complicates, but I believe it responsible for the gentling, best parts of a person's life. I am not a fool. I knew Suzie was a dog, not a human, but she had been part of our home since my sixty-fifth year. We aged together. The pages of personal essayists reflect their lives. Suzie was in the room when I wrote a dozen books and, as should be expected, appeared in all of them.

Suzie spent a decade of gay summers in Nova Scotia. For her, it was a country home. As soon as I drove through the gate and opened the car door, she jumped out and, almost shouting, dashed around the barn. She disappeared behind the hedge of rugosa roses but bounced back in sight when she crossed the side meadow and leaped onto the kitchen porch. The weeks prior to going to Four Winds always smacked of ordeals. I fretted endlessly. Would the pump work? Could the stove last another year? How about the hot water heater and the refrigerator? Had the roof leaked and more molding flaked and collapsed? Were the chimneys standing? What trees had fallen? Suppose the car broke down, and would the septic system work? Was the backhouse still intact? One year it wasn't. Suzie's enthusiasm was catching, and as I watched her race joyously, I smiled and held Vicki's hand.

This year Suzie slipped mentally, and we pondered not taking her to Canada. In the past she never barked. This spring when outdoors, she yapped unceasingly, the sound rasping and so disturbing we hurriedly let her back into the house. Once inside she chortled in an unknown tongue and wandered from room to room, bumping into chairs and walls. After what seemed only a spasm of time, she yapped to go out. Before she ate or drank, she froze and stared at her bowls. Only after Vicki and I lifted the bowls to her muzzle did she eat and drink. Caring for Suzie exhausted us. At every dinner we mentioned the unthinkable, that is, putting her to sleep. But we were cowards. Perhaps being tired and overly fond of our small stable lives weakened us. Like many an oldster, I knew my future would not be as rich as my past. As a result, I couldn't bear letting go of the sentient: a memory, a shrub I planted in the yard, and especially the "old gal." Also contributing to my inertia were Age and those false hopes which people say bloom eternally and which a person knows will never bud.

Affection isn't rational. Thank goodness. Vicki and I packed our misgivings and took Suzie to Nova Scotia. During the initial weeks when family gathered at Four Winds, minding Suzie was only one of my concerns. Often, I carried her upstairs. She was able to climb the steps. But during our first days in the house she skidded and fell twice in the downstairs hall, causing me to worry that when on the stairs she'd forget herself and fall backward. Several times a day the realization that she should go outside sounded in my head like the bell on an alarm clock. Although dementia pocked Suzie's mind, she was fit, and we leashed her and took her on our ambles, be they beach walks or strolls down the lane to pick blueberries. Her strength deceived us and made it difficult to think her old, and senile. Although I realized she would not get lost or run away, I sat on the porch steps and watched Suzie when she was outside. Sight opened the door to emotions, and as she dawdled, I...well, I felt sad.

At the end of August, Suzie suddenly worsened. She paced in circles, always clockwise. The circles varied. Some were small as the space under the kitchen table, others, large as the front parlor. She circled incessantly, once for three hours. At night she left her bed and walked circles, usually whining. We blocked the stairs with a baby gate because sometimes she spun onto the upstairs landing. Outside she ran circles. She moved so quickly that the only way I stopped her was by predicting the arc of a circle, blocking her path and grabbing her. It wasn't easy day or night. Sometimes she avoided my hands and bounding toward the house tried to jump the porch steps. She always failed banging into the second step and falling backward into the yard. I scooped her up. Cradling her in my left arm and steadying myself by holding the porch railing with my right hand, I carried her into the house. I laid her in a bed beside the kitchen table. She didn't stay. Almost immediately she resumed circling, slower than outside but tirelessly pacing, the click of her nails on the linoleum punctuating conversations with ellipses.

Besides, Vicki and me, Francis was the only family member at Four Winds at the end of August. Chew-Chums, as he called Suzie, liked and recognized him and allowed him to hold her. "She's not Suzie," he said one night as he scratched her ears. "You can't take her home. That would be cruel." Feelings made Vicki's and my feet drag. But then one afternoon as I sat outside watching Suzie circling, she suddenly stopped and, becoming immobile, shrieked in terror. I jumped from the porch, ran over, and picked her up. She was lost. That afternoon Vicki telephoned the Parade Street Animal Hospital in Yarmouth. In 2004, our first dog George was diagnosed with cancer of the mouth. He tried to eat and drink out of the side of his mouth. He wasn't successful, so one morning after a farewell walk along the bluff at the end of the lane, we took him to Yarmouth and the vet put him to sleep.

Vicki called the vet on Thursday, and after listening to Suzie's symptoms, she arranged to see her the following week. "Long enough," Vicki said, "to say goodbye." Early the next morning, the vet's office rang us. There had been a cancellation, and we were told we could bring Suzie in that afternoon. "No," Vicki moaned. "Yes," I said. I knew what to do. Eighteen years earlier I dug George's grave and buried him under the willow at the edge of the meadow. I found a flat stone in our south field, and Vicki painted "Georgie" on it. Every spring moss spread and covered the stone. Every summer I unearthed it and cleaned it. Vicki repainted the name and around it stuck whirligigs in the ground, among them a bluebird and two goldfinches.

After placing the receiver of the phone back in its cradle, I fetched a shovel, a crowbar, and a bucket from the backhouse. I carried them to the willow and four feet away from George's stone began a grave for Suzie. Both the willow and I had aged. The willow lost half its limbs, and I, my strength. After a while, my back throbbed, and I was too tired to dig standing. I removed a plastic chair from the porch, and setting it beside the hole, dug sitting down. I wedged rocks out with the crowbar, and when water seeped into the hole, I bailed with the bucket. On my finishing the grave, I lined it with sphagnum moss and switch grass to absorb additional seepage. I did an admirable job for an old guy and felt proud even as Vicki and I drove Suzie to Yarmouth. We arrived at the office early. Vicki paid the bill, $114.60, and then she and I walked Suzie around the yard. Suzie moved slowly but her coat glistened in the sunlight. "Flowering," I thought.

Eventually a technician led us inside, leaving Vicki and me in one room and taking Suzie down the hall to insert a catheter in her leg, the IV first for muscle relaxant then for pentobarbital. I didn't leave George's side at the vet's, and I hated abandoning Suzie, no matter the protocol. During the procedure George was silent. This time was different. Suzie screamed when the technician inserted the catheter. I recognized her voice. "That's Suzie. She's never been hurt before, and she's crying," I said to Vicki. "Goddamn it all to Hell!" Shortly afterward the technician returned and laid Suzie on an examining table. I was upset. I had a catch in my throat and was unable to say goodbye, but I rubbed her while the technician fed the pentobarbital into the catheter. Because Suzie was fit, the drug worked slowly, and the technician had to insert a second dose. I thought my girl would never die. Afterward, we wrapped

Suzie in a towel and drove back to Four Winds. Vicki laid her on her right side on the porch making sure her body was straight. Our other two dogs ignored her. People impose their feelings on pets. They do so despite knowing it would be unnatural for an animal to exhibit human emotions. Yet, for over fourteen years Jack, our other chihuahua mix, had not spent a night apart from Suzie. Vicki and I wanted him to feel something, and maybe he did. For the following two days, he wandered the house, going in and out of every room again and again and again.

After bringing Suzie home I rolled a wheelbarrow down the lane and using a pitchfork filled it with sphagnum. I removed the damp moss and grass from the bottom of the grave and laid down a layer of dry "bedding." Atop it I stretched Suzie, legs straight, tail curled, and her muzzle pointing toward the house. Vicki closed Suzie's eyes and wrapped her in one of her old T-shirts. Under her head she laid a heart cut from a red short-sleeved shirt advertising Bob's Surplus and given to participants in the third annual Cromwell, a ten-kilometer road race run on December 5, 1982. "She will smell us and not be lonely," Vicki said. "Not like us," I said. Vicki also put a note in the grave telling Suzie how much she'd enriched our lives and assuring her that we loved her. Finally, she put a handful of dog biscuits by Suzie's muzzle. "Easy to reach," she said. Then we scattered flowers atop Suzie so many that she was no longer visible: rose petals, New England asters, jewelweed, fall dandelions, and armfuls of goldenrod. Next, I shoveled in the dirt but none of the rocks I removed in digging the grave. Finally, I spread a thick sealing lid of sphagnum moss across the grave. I was exhausted, and that night I ate myself to sleep. I drank two Moosehead lagers and emptied two big bowls of

Vicki's soup, heavy with left over vegetables and hamburger patty. Accompanying it were slices of brown bread and a rock-sized hunk of sharp cheddar cheese. For dessert I ate vanilla ice cream, practically hidden beneath a mound of peaches, raspberries, and blueberries. I didn't talk about Suzie. She had been my old gal for too many years for glibness. The next morning I found a flat rock behind the barn. I scraped an indentation below Suzie's grave and slid the stone into it. Afterward Vicki painted "Suzie" on it. Six days later we left Nova Scotia. Hurricane Fiona prevented *The Cat* from sailing from Yarmouth, and we drove to Digby and took the ferry to Saint John. From there we drove to Augusta, Maine, and spent the night in a Comfort Inn. The next morning we returned to Storrs. "I miss her," Vicki said as we unloaded the car. "So do I," I said lifting a suitcase.

We have been home two months. Life doesn't begin at eighty. The television show was wrong. Life begins at birth. At eighty, switches are shutting down. Sometimes giant tortoises on the Galapagos Islands live a hundred and fifty years. But they eat flowers and pricky pear cactuses, don't read books, and rarely have pets. Still, since coming back to Connecticut, I have been busy, not moving quickly but lumbering about effectively. At the end of the first week, I mowed the grass, had an electrocardiogram, and resumed swimming three quarters of a mile every other day at the community center. I forgot Thoreau and at night read Turgenev. Early in October I drove to Farmington for my final shot of Lupron, ending a two-year regimen of injections. Before the first shot the doctor predicted that I'd gain twenty pounds during the treatment. "No, I won't," I said. I was wrong. "Once the effects of the final injection wear off, you'll lose weight," the doctor added. I hope he was right a second time. When the community pool is crowded, swimmers share lanes. Last week I shared a lane. "I saw a woman searching for a place to swim. Did she join you?" a man asked in the locker room. "Yes," I said. "What a thrill for her," the man said. "I expect she's always wanted to splash about with a manatee." Two kinds of silver-back males frequent the locker room, the tame who lock their lockers and the reckless who never lock theirs. The man who mentioned the manatee always locked his.

One afternoon I took Vicki to the eye doctor in West Hartford. Her uveitis wasn't active, and she didn't have to return for six months. Last week an oncologist told me, "I think we can keep you alive for as long as you want to stay alive." I laughed. He looked puzzled, but then he, too, laughed. Near the end of October, "Victoria" received an email from a medical group specializing in Alzheimer's and "Compassionate End of Life Care." "We have become aware," the email stated, "that your husband is eighty years old. We are experts in spousal support, and should the need arise (and we pray that it will not), our practice is ready to offer advice and provide therapeutic oversight." Because the elderly population has increased in recent years, the caregiver industry has boomed. "The Compassionate Invisible Fence is The Next Step in Humanitarian Senior Care Safety," declared an advertisement in a newsletter mailed to retirees. "Loving Hands, Inc." employed "state of the art" boundary technology, and its range control and rroken boundary warnings were "second to none." Moreover, a tracking option was available "for your cellphone." Individuals suffering from neurodegenerative disorders did not wear dehumanizing collars, but either anklets or wristlets, both of which were tamper and waterproof. When a wearer approached within ten yards of the fence, his anklet reacted, not shocking but tickling. If the wearer breached the fence, a siren sounded in the house, and if a caregiver purchased the company's premium plan, blue and red outdoor lights flashed.

The following week, Suzie received a birthday card advertising "chewy.com" pet food. On the front of the card appeared a cat, a dog, and a hamster, all wearing party hats. "Hi Suzie," the card read. "May today be filled with tasty treats & endless cuddles! XO Your Chewy Friends." The next day I received an email from a reviewer in England. She wanted to know in which of my books "Cash Paid for Fat Dogs" appeared. The memory forgets what the fingers wrote. A shelf of dusty books ago, I may have pasted a sign with that sentence on it to the window of a boutique butcher shop. I think I purloined the idea from one of the Peck's Bad Boy books. Hennery's antics are panaceas for the selfishness caused by youthful regimens of good behavior. Bad boys often grow up to be good men, my friend Josh maintains, while good boys frequently molder and become politicians and heartless camp followers.

Nova Scotia was far away. In the wood behind the house Jack O'Lantern mushrooms spilled over the roots of rotten trees, and bluebirds stitched across the yard resting on the hickory outside my study treating twigs like bobbins. I dreamed that Toy Toy, an imaginary cat, died. I discovered him in the front yard stretched out in the grass. Vicki and I have never had a pet cat, and I knew sight of Toy Toy would upset her, so I woke myself before she wandered into the dream and spotted him. After chlorophyll a "deserted her groves and slipped from sight," leaf blowers began tuning their instruments. Soon I joined the orchestra and cleared the yard. It took five days in the middle of which my friend Rob wrote saying, "Leaves drove me into a condominium." One afternoon something unexpected and nice happened. A man and a woman who had been blowing leaves nearby walked into the yard. "I've watched you working your ass off," the man said. "You are too old to work that hard." Afterward the man drove a massive blower across the road and blew all the leaves in the side yard into the woods. He saved me a day's work. The man refused a gratuity. He was insistent, but I am also insistent. Later, Julia, a graduate student from China, who lives nearby and everyday walks to the university library, stopped at the driveway. Julia is nice, and when she sees Vicki or me, she smiles and compliments us. "You," she said to me, "must have been handsome when you were young."

An old friend wrote that his father began working for Gulf Oil in the 1920s. He obtained leases to drill in the Emirates by giving the Sheiks Cadillacs. One of the father's compatriots had known T. E. Lawrence. James Joyce once said that imagination was memory, and as I read the account of the life of my friend's father, years slipped away, and I recalled staying in a small crumbling old hotel in Aleppo fifty years ago. Once upon a time Lawrence spent time there, and when I left the hotel, the ancient owner gave me a jar of rosebud jam. "Someday," I thought, "I will spread it across one of my white bread pages." An acquaintance in Georgia sent a sheaf of obituaries. "Well-Known Funeral Director Dies" read the caption above one announcement. A man known to be a "fine employee" worked twelve years as "a meat cutter" at Kroger. Afterward he spent many years "employed by the M. P. Latham Funeral Home." "I assume," Vicki said, "that he didn't begin as an apprentice at Latham's." Named among Little Belle's survivors along with her husband, children, and grandchildren were two former male friends whose "favors she enjoyed before marriage took her out of the game." Othniel Braxton manufactured plastic facsimiles of human organs. These could be purchased singly or in conjunction with other abdominal viscera. Ottie was also a devoted gardener, and to "keep his thumbs green" sold "doctor planters," ceramic likenesses of body parts. Thus, a dentist might buy a white porcelain molar six inches tall and five wide into the indented crown of which a small plant could be inserted. Ottie produced a line of such planters. His obituary mentioned ears and fingers and noted that the ceramics were popular with specialists. The account did not mention a planter that would appeal to proctologists, but Ottie lived in Dalton, and reading that a citizen of north Georgia produced such an item would not have surprised me. If Ottie did so, it would have been the most popular planter in his therapeutic greenhouse, at least among men raised in the South.

"Did someone really mail you those last two obituaries?" Vicki said. "Maybe, but my memory is poor, and I lie a lot. Lies are antidotes for reality," I replied, bending over to pick up Jack and carry him outside. Jack's kidneys are failing. He sleeps most of the day and probably won't survive winter. "Next summer should we go to Four Winds in June or wait until July as we did this year?" Vicki asked. "I contacted a man to pump out the septic tank." "I don't know," I said. "I feel so damn tired." "Writing will buck you up. 'To write is to be alive,'" Vicki said, emending Thoreau's well-known proscriptive maxim. I swallow too many pills every morning for me to dislocate my jaw and bolt aphorisms. Still, Vicki was right. Winter is almost here, and I've decided to force myself into bloom and write about budding spring times, those of place and of life. If I put chrysanthemums in my hair, maybe I'll remember some "gentle people." Certainly, I'll ramble here and there, hither and thither, and up and down the page. A straight line is the shortest distance between two points, Charles Conrad Abbott acknowledged. But, he added, "it is not in favor" because "it reduces life to too simple an equation." After finishing, I will inter what I have written. All scribblers worth the price of ink should leave behind unpublished manuscripts. Rationally they know the papers will disappear. Nevertheless, corpses-to-be can enliven their death beds and titillate themselves by imagining the manuscripts exploding into print and causing hullabaloos.

6

Idling

Idlers regulate timing belts on automobile engines. In people, time regulates idling. Youth can choose to be idle. Idleness is imposed upon the old. Age establishes speed limits, and no matter how close to the floorboard, people of a certain age press their gas pedals, their motors won't accelerate. Being idle determines perception. "America seems a good country if a person never leaves home," a retired friend remarked recently. Out of the house my friend thinks differently. "Whenever I enter a grocery or drugstore or a doctor's waiting room, I look around and decide how I will behave and where I will go if someone comes in carrying a gun. The nation is addicted to violence, and there are more congregants who kiss gunstocks than there are Methodists." "As a result," my friend continued, "I'm idling away these last years barricaded behind closed doors." Three weeks ago, driving home from Hartford, I stopped at Dunkin' Donuts in Coventry. I ordered two coconut doughnuts to give to Vicki. While I stood at the counter, a man came in wearing a pistol. The grip jutted out loosely from a holster at the man's mid-drift. The man was unkempt and looked like something the cat sucked and spat out. I put a five-dollar bill on the counter and left the store before the clerk fetched my doughnuts. I am not as retiring as the friend who locks himself in his house, but I won't return to Dunkin' Donuts in Coventry.

Age exacerbates anchoritic inclinations. But in truth only the willfully unobservant think now is America's best of times. It is not the worst of times, but if one's hearing is historically acute, he may hear rumblings of the eve of destruction. Certainly, my friend is a worry collector and isn't happy unless something is nagging him. But he is also radio-shocked. Radio shatters quiet and peace of mind and depopulates the listener's world. It drives away colorful and imaginary characters before they get up to something interesting and replaces them with cardboard cutouts. My friend switches the radio on when he wakes in the morning and listens to the news throughout the day, in the evening supplementing it with television. I suspect he would be more at ease away from home and less apprehensive if he suffered a therapeutic hearing loss. For my part I am not a news hound. Certainly, I don't ramble footloose and concern-free as I once did. But my idleness and reclusiveness reflect age more than social awareness. Because my days are not bracketed by schedule, I devote much time to enduring nuisances.

I don't own a snowblower or pay a plowman to clean my drive after a winter storm. I shift the snow myself. I lift and toss, and the hours pass slowly. Cars stream by on Hillside Circle headed for the university, but I hardly notice them. I try to fool myself into believing I am the robust guy I once was. I fail, but failure between the garage and the two unused newspaper holders beside the sidewalk doesn't amount to much. After I finish shoveling, I go into the kitchen and pull off my boots and heavy wool sweater. I hang my gloves and stocking cap on the back of the closet door in the pantry. Afterward, I brew a pot of tea, and if the container hasn't been hidden on some dark shelf below my ability to bend and reach, I scoop up a couple of spoonsful of peanut butter. I then sit down at the kitchen table and thumb a wildlife magazine. I don't read the copy. I only look at pictures, all of which vanish almost before I see them. If Vicki comes into the room, I complain about pain in my lower back and hips. "You are a damn fool. You are too old to shovel snow. Someday you'll have a heart attack. You'll fall out dead in the driveway, and I won't discover your body until it's frozen solid," she says, a statement that I find very appealing. I then drink the dregs of my tea, limp into the study, and sitting in my reading chair fall asleep, making the morning unremarkably satisfactory.

The other outdoor winter nuisance to which I devote time is picking up sticks and tossing them atop the woodpile behind the house. Once, I raced across the yard raking sticks. After a morning's work the ground was bare as a baby's backside in a talcum powder advertisement. Afterward the afternoon was free for other things. Now other things are few, and I move slowly, my back creaking when I lean over. I pause often, and cleaning the yard takes three days, after which March winds generally force me to start again. With my idler going full blast, that is, slowing my pace to a creep, I notice things ignored in the past. Forty years ago, I bought a red cart in which to haul sticks and rocks into the wood behind the house. Not until this year when I was sitting on a granite outcrop in the backyard did I read the writing on the side of the cart. Then I learned I owned a Jackson Yard Cart No. 16, produced by Jackson Manufacturing in Harrisburg, Pennsylvania. "What do you think about that?" I asked Vicki later when I was resting in the kitchen. "I'm speechless," Vicki said. "That's the safest thing to be nowadays," I said.

My son Edward and I correspond about books. In my last letter I urged him to reread *Tom Jones* before life became too heavy for zest. "Fielding" I said, "makes me wistful for lost imaginative possibilities. His pages kindle visions of daylight moments warm with the joy of spontaneity. All too soon, mental and physical pains seep into life and canker gaiety." I confessed that I did not spend as much time reading as in the past. Instead, I idled away hours listening to sentimental songs purple with melancholy, grapes amenable to the aged palate and good ear food for dozing. Tomorrow, the weatherman says snow will be "on the grass again," I continued and recommended he listen to "Lorena" and "When You and I were Young, Maggie," two of my afternoon favorites. In reply, Edward said he'd begun rereading Fielding. "But, gee," he wrote, "you need an injection of levity. Go downtown. Don't buy any doughnuts but bounce around. Be a bit yeasty. Have you considered taking helium? Or smoking dope? What about a marathon viewing of 'Jeeves and Wooster'? Dad, have you accepted Jesus Christ as your Lord and Savior?"

In the study I often lay down my pen and idle through "work time" birdwatching. Last week a small flock of bluebirds beat across the yard, pausing and momentarily alighting on low branches. A brown tree creeper scratched around an oak digging into crevices in the bark. A pileated woodpecker foraged across broken trees behind the house, and a broad-tailed hawk settled hunched in a hickory, from the front resembling a brown and white barred Buddha. "Don't look through a hole in the fence," an old maxim warns, "you may not like what you see." For people my age the future is known and grimly realistic. In contrast, the past is a place of miracles. When Edward and Erica were anticipating the birth of a child, Vicki turned away from the fence and glancing backward wrote them in South Carolina. "Eliza," Vicki reminisced, "recently sent a photo of daffies blooming in California, and I imagine they must be poking through your neighborhood, too. Would that we could say the same up here in cold old New England. But I am so glad you will be welcoming a new baby as spring's blossoms and shoots unfurl. I remember looking out the car window at the white blossoming trees on Mansfield City Road as Dad drove newborn Francis and me home from the hospital, and it was magical. I've always remembered that. May you have magical moments—too many to count—in the days to come. Spring, birth, and rebirth—a time to cherish." I, too, remember that drive, and as I sit unmoving in the silent study, magical moments thrust through the arid ground of decades, tears of remembrance watering them and making them shoot. Idleness is a finger pointing toward the fading past. It enables a person to see the forgotten and endow it with new life, indeed endow the person himself with the awareness that he lived.

I should have told Edward that I no longer read "meaty" books. I avoid thoughtful volumes that disrupt calm and cause insomnia. In libraries I shun tomes which readers complete out of a malformed sense of duty, having been educated into embracing the falsehood that people should finish what they start. No, most books I read are so insignificant I forget the titles before beginning the first chapters. They don't make critical demands. I can lay them aside and reopen or not reopen them according to whim. I suppose that from the perspective of the indoctrinating present and the wide-awake who hoe though pages searching for the inappropriate, portions of the books I've read in the new year are reprehensible. However, as an idler, I am immune to ardor. For me, the books are entertainments akin to sawdust-trail circuses. Moreover, I am the single member of my book club. The club's selections are idiosyncratic and unread by anyone I know, or, indeed, will ever know. Recently, I read four of Captain or, as his rank changed, Lt. Colonel Frederick S. Brereton's books. For boys Brereton wrote some forty adventure novels, most published in the first three decades of the twentieth century. Akin to G. A. Henty's swashbuckling fiction, Brereton's plots were rambunctious with derring-do, improbable transformations, and good thunking fights and battles. Accounts of the number of Brereton's books differ. I read four because that was all I found in the university stacks. Looking for more would have necessitated effort or forced me to read online and strain my eyes and back. Moreover, like a sip of "country" Champagne, a sample was pleasure enough.

Scouts of the Baghdad Patrols was the first of Brereton's books I read. When I found the volume in a neglected corner of the library, I expected to thumb only the initial page. My days of playing in a sandbox ended in kindergarten, and I suspected the high jinks of adolescent boys would be as arid as the Syrian Desert, no matter the merit badges they earned. I was wrong. The beginning paragraph awakened childhood dreams of adventures. After boys disappear into men, they lay aside tales of bravado and valor. In evenings of satisfactory domesticity, they read mysteries like *Case of the Nasty Man*, a bestseller in Norway in the 1920s, "the wintriest book ever written by a Laplander," a reviewer in *Tidens Tigna* judged. Later after families and responsibilities fray, old boys enjoy clarity more than puzzles. Often they return to simple childhood reading, straightforward entertainments that palliate regimens of pills. Instead of lamenting roads not taken, they read about roads impossible to take even in imagination. "Michael Dent," *Scouts* began,

> stood beside the rail of the river steamer, listening unconsciously to the gentle thud of the paddles and peering ahead in the eager endeavor to pierce the thin mist which overhung the muddy, oily surface of the Mighty Tigris River. Somewhere ahead, hugging the bank lay Baghdad, his destination; Baghdad, the mysterious city, with its teeming thousands of people: Turks, Armenians, Arabs, Persians, Europeans, dusky inhabitants of every sort, Jews, Christians, and Mohammedans.

After watching Dent for a paragraph, I grabbed a tow rope woven out of sentences and pulled myself aboard the steamer. Although Dent disembarked at Baghdad, I stowed away, and remaining on board sailed into the mist, not disembarking until I finished *Scouts* and the other three of Brereton's books I found.

On this initial leg of my journey, meeting "rogues, thieves, vagabonds, and restless beggars," as well as "robbers, ruffians, and cutthroats" so pleased me that for two afternoons I neglected to walk downtown and drink senior cups of coffee at Dog Lane Café. Cutthroats were an especially dangerous and common species of villain, and acquaintances warned the scouts that "Allah blesses the man who slits the throat of an infidel." Although hardened malefactors were beyond redemption, scouting offered hope for the malleable. Dent's uncle believed that "many a noble heart" beat under the unprepossessing appearance of many "brats" in Baghdad. "If they could be caught young and trained young, and fine ideas could be pumped into their heads at the impressionable age," he opined, "they might grow up honest, decent, gallant citizens, unharmed by other influences which normally surround them." Such influences don't make copy as exciting as gunfights, pursuits on horse and camelback, near killings, battles in ancient ruins, and then wondrously exhilarating, the escape of "Mick" and "Jack" from a mahela, a small riverboat. A band of rogues grabbed the boys, bound them, and tossed them into the hold of the boat. The abductors intended to transport them far from Baghdad and drown them where their bodies wouldn't immediately be discovered. In addition to the boys, the mahela carried a cargo of corpses in transit for burial. As experienced readers could anticipate, the Baghdad Scouts escaped their predicament by taking the motto "Be Prepared" to hand and heart. Mick and Jack commandeered a coffin and lowering it over the side of the mahela drifted away from their captors and back into the scout troop. The coffin was not a vessel conventional adults would find enticing. But it was a yacht certain to appeal to lively boys and to men who had aged beyond the confines of their stolid middle years, especially if the initial occupant of the coffin were still in residence and hadn't bloated so much that he resembled a pillow and cramped the casket making joining him difficult.

On the rooster of the leading scouts were Mick, Tom, Bruce, Jack, Sandy, Norman, and Effan, topping lads, enough to constitute the line of a championship high school football team. "Burly" Jack being the center, and the speedy split end, Effan, a Welshman whose actual name was Evan Williams. Not only did Evan convince his "teammates" to give him a playing-field nickname, but he was wiry, intelligent, and had "an untidy crop of hair clinging to his forehead," this last hinting that he was fleet afoot, not the "lad" to allow a mousse to plaster him out of innovation. The three most treacherous villains were Selim, Mahmud, and Assol. The pronunciation of this last name so eluded me that I dared not say it in polite company, certainly not in the presence of peacharines, in truth not something I fretted about because in Brereton's four books there were just five or six females, two of which only made last page cameo appearances as wives.

Markings on old volumes ripple beyond story like the waves caused by throwing a stone into a still pond. In a small way they endow a book with life and increase the pleasure of reading. *Scouts* was published in 1921. Printed by hand in tall black letters on the front endpaper was "New Year 1922." Underneath at a later date, J. Kendall wrote his name in pencil. Inside, between page 244 and the plate showing Jake and Mike lowering themselves from the mahela into the casket was a bookmark, the top of a page ripped out of a magazine, a seven and three quarter by three- and three-quarter-inch strip folded into eighths. On the bookmark an ancient stone bridge spanned a river. The river swept to the left and disappeared. On the dry bank directly under the bridge stretched a farm field, at the far edge a fence, behind it a large stone house, probably a combination of barn, backhouse, and home. "Maybe the Dordogne River Valley in France," I thought, a place which I had never seen and never would see. Why do such things matter? In a large sense, they don't. But people don't live in large senses. They live amid tidbits that flavor days.

Stamped on the title page of Brereton's *With Shield and Assegai* "A Tale of the Zulu War" was "John McFarlane. Mount Mascal Gds. Bexley Kent." Twice on two other pages, T. Keable stamped his name and "Mount Masca Farm. North Cray. Kent." Deciphering the print was difficult. While one stamp was upside down, letters were missing from both. Perhaps older readers are as intrigued by the mist surrounding stories as much as by the tales themselves. After the conclusion of *With Shield and Assegai* appeared sixteen pages advertising and describing "Blackie & Son's Illustrated Story Books." On the title page of *With Shield*, Blackie listed offices in London, Glasgow, and Dublin. The title pages of other books included Bombay and Toronto. Henty wrote thirty-one of Blackie's books. Beside twenty-two of them someone had drawn a line, an eighth of an inch long in ink. I don't know whether the line marked volumes owned, read, or those the marker anticipated reading. When I was a boy, I kept records of the books I read, for example twenty-six of the Hardy Boys novels. Decades later I listed the plays I saw. I assume that other boys also recorded books. But again, maybe not. Aside from places like the Blackie & Son advertisement, I never met a literary boy like me much less tracked him through a catalogue.

Before closing *With Shield*, I read the descriptions of Henty's books. *Condemned as a Nihilist* described the travails of a young Englishman exiled to Siberia after being involved in "political plots" in St. Petersburg. After several abortive attempts to escape, he made his way home, the journey perilous and lasting two years. In *With Kitchener in the Soudan*, the hero "displays so much dash and enterprise that he soon attains an exceptionally high rank for his age." He played a distinguished part in all "the military operations," and "adventure follows so close on adventure that the end of the story is reached all too soon." Listed among Blackie's other publications were six of Brereton's novels, the only one of which attracted me being *With the Dyaks of Borneo*. Tyler won a commission "by a gallant act" and was on the way to join his ship in Borneo when he was "set upon by a band of Malay and Dyak pirates." After escaping he became "the leader of a tribe of head-hunting Dyaks." Tyler then led his mates through deep forests "towards Sarawak" on the way defeating the pirates. Later, he experienced many adventures and hard fighting until being "disabled by a wound." Among Blackie's publications were a sampling of novels by seventeen other writers. The single one that almost intrigued me was Herbert Strang's *Brown of Moukden*, an account of the Russo-Japanese War "from the Russian side," a companion to his *Kolo* which depicted the war from the Japanese side.

Jones of the 64th "A Tale of the Battles of Assaye and Laswaree" was the second of Brereton's books I read. It was a rambunctious stew thick with an abandoned baby, bullies, a foundling home, a typhoon, vicious rhinoceroses in Sumatra, land pirates, cantankerous beggars in Calcutta, and blood running like water through open faucets. Most of the tale occurred in India amid the British Empire's endless conflicts. In part the narrative was a Horatio Alger story as Jones rose from anonymity and poverty through grit, courage, and decency to become Sir Owen Marshall "possessor of a very fine fortune in England." However, the climb was harsh and at times painful as Jones was wounded several times. Indeed, before becoming landed, he lost his right arm. Heroes in Brereton's novels had trouble avoiding amputations. In *With Wellington in Spain*, Tom Clifford escaped criminal impressment in the navy after which he joined Wellington's soldiery and eventually became the youngest colonel in the army. On the way to becoming a member of Wellington's staff, he, too, lost an arm although Brereton did not specify the particular "wing."

Also adding to their attraction was that Brereton's volumes felt like good value. Pages were thick and the covers hard bound. *With Wellington* and *Scouts* were handfuls, the former measuring seven and three-quarter by six inches, its 380 pages forming a two-inch pile. The latter was eight by six inches, the pile of its pages one and three-quarter inches. Decorated, the hard covers of Brereton's books caught the eye and the imagination. Bursting shouting out of the red cover of *With Shield* was a Zulu warrior in full battle dress, his right hand raised above his head shaking an assegai (spear with an iron blade), in his left a large shield stitched together out of brown and white animal hides. On his head he wore a cap adorned with a single horn and two feathers. The remnants of a lion's mane hung wind-blown from under the cap looking like blonde untrimmed locks sliced from a weather woman's wig. Tied around the warrior's right wrist, his knees, and around his neck like a feathery gorget were other blonde remnants. The warrior's feet were abnormally long and flat, leading me to suspect he might have been the book's hero Donald Stewart in disguise. Stewart spent his early years in Zululand. On returning to Britain for school, he ran afoul of a bully who besmirched his reputation. Consequently, he joined the army and returned to South Africa. Once there while fighting in the Zulu wars, he discovered his sister had been kidnapped by unscrupulous natives. Befitting a Brereton hero, he set out to rescue her dressed as a native warrior. A surgeon who tended to one of his battle wounds helped his disguise by giving him "some stuff in a bottle" used by actors to dye themselves. Steward was successful in part because he spoke Zulu as a child. Similarly, the Hindustani which Jones of the 64th learned as a toddler and recalled only after becoming a soldier contributed to his success in India.

After the Zulu War, Stewart returned to Britain and enrolled in medical school at the University of Edinburgh. Bloodletting and soldiering had become ingrained in his character, and after marrying, he became an army doctor and "served with British troops in various parts of the world." Although Stewart probably amputated a barrow of limbs, he eluded the misfortune of Marshall and Clifford and did not lose an arm himself. Excessive easy chair adventuring is not as risky to elderly idlers as brigands and warfare were to the young heroes of Brereton's books. At its worst, extended immobile hours may occasion backside and leg cramps. Additionally, some people believe that reading affects behavior. Such folks waste their days and those of others discovering then diagnosing causes and effects. "An unrelieved regimen of children's adventure novels might cause a hitch in an oldster's step," an educational psychologist opined, "leading an ancient boy to jump a little and act 'boldly.'" As reluctant as I am to agree with any species of psychologist, that is what happened to me. Shortly after closing the book on Tom Clifford's lively doings, I received a bill from the Town of Mansfield. The bill stated that the payment of my yearly property taxes was a penny short and as a result assessed a two-dollar penalty, claiming I owed the town $2.01. In Mansfield a taxpayer can pay his yearly taxes in two halves, one half due the first of July, the second, the first of January. In both instances the property owner has thirty days in which to pay the installment, thus he can delay paying the January installment until the end of the month. Dated February 13, the letter from the town noted that the grace period for paying the penny had expired. It also informed me that after fifteen days (February 1–15), I would owe a second two dollars.

The strident behavior of Brereton's boys influenced my response to the bill. Instead of meekly handing over the $2.01, I exclaimed, "what in Hell kind of crap is this?" I didn't wave an assegai in defiance, but I told Vicki that only a chickenshit would pay the two dollars. On the previous June 22, I paid the entirety of my yearly tax bill, that is, both the first and second halves. A clerk in the tax office computed the amount, took my check, and gave me a receipt stamped "paid in full." If there were a one-penny error, it was the clerk's, not mine. Although I paid the full assessment for the sake of convenience, payment of the second half of the bill wasn't due until January 1. In school I had been an adept and creative mathematician. I enjoyed finding round-about, mind-tickling ways to prove geometry theorems. Class sizes were large, and not all teachers appreciated gothic ornateness. But, no matter, I did. How dreary existence would be if everything plodded straight from point A to point B without a genial detour to D or F, and if a person were a real sport, to luscious S and perhaps to T although setting up shop under the arm of this last letter was always "dicey."

As childhood knowledge of Zulu furthered Donald Stewart's military career, so in contesting the two-dollar fine, I resuscitated my penchant for innovative mathematics. I noted that half my yearly property taxes amounted to $3,258. Although this half of my payment was not due until January 1, 2023, the town accepted my money on June 22, 2022. However, it neglected to pay me interest on what in effect was an advance payment. Instead, "the town pocketed the interest without even a thank-you." To repeat: on February 13, 2023, the town fined me two dollars for being late on my taxes. The fine was for the first fifteen days of February and was scheduled to increase by two dollars every fifteen days until "full payment of the penny" was received. In a letter I handed both to the town manager and to the collector of revenue, I observed that the second half of 2022, from the beginning of July to the end of December, was approximately 180 days or twelve fifteen-day increments. For the twelve increments, I calculated, the town "owes me twenty-four dollars, that is, twelve times two." But that, of course, was only the top line of Mansfield's liability. The bottom line amounted to more. I noted that the $3,258 payment consisted of 325,800 pennies, not a single penny, which at Town Hall that morning I paid with a shiny Honest Abe and for which I demanded and received a receipt. Applying the town's slippery slide rule to the pennies, I concluded Mansfield owed me $24 multiplied by 325,800 for a grand total of $7,819,200. The following Monday I received a letter rescinding the two-dollar fine. In return I "graciously" dropped my claim for the seven, damn near, eight million simoleons. The expenses of idlers are modest. Moreover, they treasure calm, and that much dough would have given me a conniption fit. "Well," Vicki said later, "They won't forget you in Town Hall. If you go over there again, you'll find all the doors closed and every employee out to lunch."

"You bet your ass. That's the way I like things," I said after which I fetched a chocolate croissant from the kitchen and stretched out in my easy chair. I purged the off-the-page vernacular used by Tom Clifford's compatriots in the Forlorn Hope at Badajoz. My language improved rapidly. To describe digestive siroccos, never again would I mouth the four-letter word beginning with an *f*, ending in a *t*, and popularized by Old English ruffians. After stripping the crudity from my vocabulary, I donned a hazmat suit and adopted the volcanologists' scientific "outgassed." Dozy hours lend themselves to linguistic refinement. Last week during an advertising break between parts of *Sanditon* on television, Vicki announced she'd scrubbed the phrase "liquor store" from her speech. "It has a loutish appearance and a gagging oleaginous sound," she said, declaring that henceforth she intended to use the rounded, semi-formal "alcohol shop."

Later that night, I began the first chapter of *Case of the Nasty Man*. I glimpsed a reindeer and spotted blood drops on the snow leading into a copse of white birch trees. But I didn't get a chance to search beneath the trees. Edward telephoned from South Carolina and announced the birth of Mikey, Sammy Pickering's older younger brother. Mikey weighed in at a robust eight and a half pounds. Three years before Sammy made his appearance, a doctor froze five of Erica and Edward's fertilized eggs. The invasive machinations of anti-abortionists brought the eggs to mind, and Erica and Edward had them analyzed. Four were compromised, but one was viable. Although the doctor wasn't optimistic about the egg's taking, much less reaching term, he implanted it. Children under eighteen were not admitted into Erica's hospital. The morning after Mikey's birth while driving Sammy to day care, Edward showed him a photograph of Erica with Mikey beside her in the bed. "Oh, Mommy," Sammy said then noticing Mikey, exclaimed "baby" after which he burst into tears.

The two boys are Vicki's and my only grandchildren. Because I am an octogenarian and Edward and Erica live nine hundred and thirty highway miles away from Storrs, I won't see the children often. For me they will be paper rather than flesh and bone grandchildren. But I am happy. Vicki is eleven years younger than me. She will have many opportunities to know and love them, and during the time remaining to me, I will nap in my easy chair. I'll imagine the boys' hands in mine. Together we'll wander the fields and hills of dreams. The sky above us will be blue and gold. We'll pick blackberries and wild strawberries. Old Mr. Porcupine will trundle past waving his quills. Curly the Snake will slide through the grass. Jumpy the Shrew will look out the window of his log home and see us. Johnny Loon will laugh, and then, as it must, day will end. dark will spread softly across the horizon. Good night, the mourning dove, will sing, and that will be that.

7

Sapient

"Ah, Mr. Childress, what will you be working on this summer?" Professor Bowbidge said, on meeting my friend John Childress in Firestone Library at the end of spring semester. John planned to write a dissertation on Malcolm Lowry, known for his Herculean consumption of alcohol and the novel *Under the Volcano*. Lowry wrote the novel in Mexico in the late 1930s. "I intend to study the oeuvre of several artists who lived and wrote in or about Mexico during the 1920s and 30s. I anticipate their works functioning as compasses, directing me to the creative strata which erupted and formed the *Volcano*. Among the authors whose works I will peruse are D. H. Lawrence and Harry Franck, the travel writer. I will also examine the art of Frida Kahlo, and perhaps that of Diego Rivera to whom Frida, among others, was married." John's response would have given me virulent turgidity. An old courser, Professor Bowbidge was made of hardier stuff. He raised his right eyebrow into an arc and said, "Sapient, Mr. Childress, sapient."

Although I read *Under the Volcano*, I remember nothing about it. What I recall are Childress, Professor Bowbidge, and "sapient." In graduate school criticism was acidic with wood pulp. Unlike anecdotes fashioned out of rough, indeed ragged, behavior, the pulp eventually shredded and vanished. As a person ages, he realizes that marginalia endure longer than signatures of pages dense and trussed with analysis. Days themselves become parchments of small matters. Eventually the particulars of memorable moments become hazy. What remains and becomes storied recollection are marginalia. Rarely do I write about political matters. Recent conduct of gun-venerating Republicans in the Tennessee legislature has been searing and reprehensible. Time, of course, will muddy the details of their actions. What I will recall and probably repeat, or at least think about repeating, is a bit of marginalia, a comment in a letter from my friend Josh. "Those Tennessee Republicans all need purgative doses of the old-fashioned rodenticide 'Rough on Rats.' It should be administered as a suppository, just the way real assholes like it." "Sapient," I responded. "Sapient."

Marginalia enlightened ancient, illuminated manuscripts. They decorated and emphasized. They awakened appreciation and lightened reading. They made the contents of, say, a psalter more memorable than the volume would have seemed had it been a clump of unadorned pages. Three days a week I swim two-thirds of a mile at the town community center. The mind erases most locker-room conversations before they are spoken—chat about pets, grandchildren, sensible suicides, and cancers so common they seem domesticated, these last most often prostate and pancreatic. Occasionally, however, a statement is so red that its words seemed compounded out of brazilwood and madder roots. "I've dressed and undressed in this room for a decade, and I have yet to see a goosing," Fred said one morning after "Water Fitness" class. "That's because most people hereabouts are atheists," Burt replied. "If they were Pentecostals from your old state Alabama, there is no telling what would occur." "Waking turns people our age into atheists," Fred opined. "Only masochists could believe in a deity that condemns the elderly to the agony of hellish morning after hellish morning then sentences them to enduring days without parole."

Much marginalia is blue, not the sharp blue of azurite, but the pale, pastel blue of duplicity. Sometimes the guile is so cack-handed that ignoring it without marveling is difficult. Recently Mrs. Zongo Kari emailed me. She was, she recounted, "a dying woman here in the hospital, I was diagnosed as a Cancer patient over 2 years ago. I am a business woman dealing with Gold Exploration. I Am from Us California. I have a charitable and unfulfillment project that am about to hand over to you. If you are interested please Reply, hope to hear from you." "Aside from being profane rather than sacred, the recompense offered by Mrs. Zongo," Josh declared after reading the email, "differs little from the promises dangled before people who perused illuminated religious texts. Don't forget that living is smoother for true believers than for skeptics." I don't think Josh was correct. Certainly, financial life has not been smooth for another of my email correspondents, "Aisha Al-Qaddafi, the only biological Daughter of Former President of Libya Col. Muammar Al-Qaddafi." Aisha was a refugee and a widow with three children. Because she did not understand the workings of a "free" economy, she was running low on cash and desperately needed a savvy American, someone like me, to help her invest twenty-seven and a half million dollars.

Days are composed of marginalia. On Sunday Vicki and I ate breakfast in the Aero Diner in North Windham. Afterward I wandered into the All Pets Club next door. I quickly learned that reptiles interested the manager. On my mentioning that the single disappointment of a trip last year to the West Coast was not seeing a California kingsnake, the manager led me into a back room. White and black, their scales glistening and sliding silently and polished, California kingsnakes are lovelier than strings of flawless South Sea pearls. I disapprove, nay loathe, the pet trade in animals; yet, my heart bounded when the manager showed me a young California kingsnake. Later, the thought of natural beauty's being trapped in an aquarium brought my mood down, as did driving back to Mansfield and seeing two opossums in the middle of Storrs Road, their lives reduced to humps. "Both female," Vicki said.

Days are mixed. Some of the marginalia is asphalt and dead. Others are green and vital. Soon after arriving home from breakfast, Vicki and I walked across the university grounds. Daphne was flowering, and its fragrance drifted across the campus, the perfume redolent of a blissful imagined Eternity. The small yellow magnolias behind the library were in full bloom. Their scent was mild, and to appreciate it Vicki and I leaned into the trees almost losing our balance amid the blossoms. That afternoon Vicki went to Big Y. In the bottom of her grocery basket lay a page torn from a pink notepad on which was written a shopping list. The list was modest, and the letters of the items trembled across the paper making the shopper seem feeble, probably at the beginning of the Parkinson's stage of life. Following apples, cheese, "1 lime, cookies, hot cross buns, milk, eggs 6" were "O J" [orange juice], apple sauce, muffins, whiffer pads, and dish soap. Last on the list were "4 Depends" and "TP" [toilet paper]. Only one item was undecipherable. The letters appeared to spell "cot." Because "cot" followed milk and eggs, I guessed it stood for cottage cheese.

Not only do bits and pieces shape the fabric of paragraphs and days, but they resuscitate the forgotten. Collections of marginalia are the stuff of which biographies are made. Large bookish calendars deceive by creating the illusion of enduring, abiding events. Years with their front and back matter, their seemingly imperishable hard covers, vanish overnight. In the early seventies, I lived in Amman, Jordan, for a year. Last month an acquaintance asked what life there was like. I recalled almost nothing. I couldn't describe where I lived, shopped, or what I ate or read. That evening after looking at the marginalia in the living room, I remembered more. "Yes, I was there," I thought, noticing David Roberts's prints of Petra hanging on the wall and the massive Mother-of-Pearl dowry chest filling a dark side of the room. The chest was four feet long, a foot and a half wide, and three and a half tall, large enough for an attic of memories. But, alas, I couldn't remember where I bought the chest. I recollected visiting Petra twice, but how did I get there I wondered, and where did I stay? I think I slept in a cave, but I'm not sure.

I taught at the University of Jordan, but I have no idea what I taught. "Living," Vicki said when the blank in my memory bothered me. "Living," she continued, "that's all you've ever taught. You were damn good at it. The subjects didn't matter. Each year and in each place, the courses changed, but the lessons remained the same." Scattered through the volumes I wrote decades ago are anecdotes describing my experiences in Jordan. Reading the books would probably revive pieces of that year. But on the other hand, it might not. Last month at the Mansfield Library book sale, I found a copy of *Still Life*, a collection of my essays published in 1990. The essays were a familiar blend of the serious and comic and described portions of my thoughts and life in the late 1980s. I bought the book for a dollar. I should have paid a hundred dollars. That would have boosted my local reputation. I can hear the talk now. "My god, someone paid $100 for one of Sam Pickering's books. I didn't realize how valuable his writing is. We have underestimated him for years." In any case the volume I purchased had not been opened. I flipped through a handful of pages. The *I* in the chapters and the life he led had almost disappeared. I considered reading the book. I didn't. Instead, I turned it into contemporary marginalia. During the past year, dieback stripped greenery from the life of a distant correspondent. In the 80s and 90s, I often strayed from the main texts of essays and illuminated margins with happy yellow tales, the color not fashioned from crocus flowers but from countrified stamens. I hoped the tales would make readers smile. I thought doing so wise and decent, indeed sapient. The morning after the book sale, I mailed *Still Life* to my correspondent in hopes that for a moment a story would brighten his mood.

The past often disappears while a person observes the present. Last month the university started tearing down the Mansfield Apartments. The buildings were brick and solid and comfortable. Sidewalks ran between them and around large companionable lawns. Vicki and I lived there our first years in Storrs. Each apartment had a separate entrance. All were two stories high and joined side by side resembled modest blocks of townhouses. Our apartment consisted of four rooms, a small kitchen and living room downstairs and two bedrooms upstairs. Francis was born while we lived there, and we knew more people in Storrs then than we have at any time since. For two months wrecking has ground through days, bulldozers scraping and pushing, cranes hovering, and the shovels of excavators plunging like the bills of carrion-feeding birds. Behind a fence on the South Eagleville Road are tangles of wire and jagged mounds of shingles, concrete, cinder blocks, wood, and aluminum. Noise of the destruction reverberates off the Community Center across the road, and when Vicki and I drive past, sometimes I imagine Melanie Safka singing "Look What They Have Done to My Song, Ma." The words are slightly different; *my song* has become *our past*. On the table in the kitchen is a ceramic tile Vicki and I bought sometime somewhere in Greece. In the middle is 77, the number of our old apartment. Decades ago, the tile fell off the table and broke in half. Vicki glued it back together. Now the effort seems metaphoric, a futile attempt to preserve the past, to mend the inevitable breakages of time.

Familiar places and lives associated with them are fated to become refuse. Family farms are sold and transformed into malls and subdivisions. The Nashville of my childhood is now another place, "Nashvegas." If I returned for a visit, I would be a stranger. Reading pages of the past, the thick texts of my years in Old Nashville would confuse me and quickly become an ordeal. My life exists in the marginalia of *now*, anecdotes sometimes significant but usually not, silly doings that glitter for a moment. Afterward their colors fade and their paint chips and flakes, but for a brief present they are vital and true and are my life. Last month in the kitchen, Vicki startled me by exclaiming, "you are so boring!" She said it six times. For a while I'd been singing a stanza from the "Polly Wolly Doodle" song: "A grasshopper sitting on a railroad track / Singing Polly Wolly Doodle all day, / A-picking his teeth with a carpet tack, / Singing Polly Wolly Doodle all day." I cannot recall the number of times I'd repeated the stanza. But it was more than a handful, not enough to disturb a rational stranger but perhaps sufficient to irritate a wife preparing dinner. Vicki's outburst morphed into a discussion of being opinionated followed by dinner's being delayed while she telephoned our daughter Eliza. "Daddy says that I am the most opinionated person he knows whereas he is broad-minded and not in the least assertive," Vicki said. "Because of female solidarity, you will agree with Mom," I interrupted addressing Eliza, "and since I am forbearing, bias won't bother me." "I can assure you," Eliza answered, "that my thought on the matter is completely gender-neutral and nonbinary." Before I responded, she continued, "I'd say you are both opinionated about different things at different times." "Being opinionated is a defining family trait. But," she continued raising her voice into the emphatic, "Daddy is definitely extremely opinionated." Eliza's refusal to seize bullheadedness by the horns and calibrate the extent of her mother's penchant for dogmatism further delayed dinner and led to an after-telephone conversation colorful with equine traits, that is, of mules and donkeys, especially male donkeys. Eventually Vicki shouted, "Mute Game," a phrase which in our house commands silence without being rude.

Equating minor domestic matters to iconographic illustrations in medieval psalters may strike people whose visions are narrowly academic as wrong-headed. But so what, so darn what? Not to leap fences and tumble over the rails of definitions and topic sentences are to deny possibilities, and vitality itself. Nevertheless, the earliest and most famous illuminations were in books, not kitchens. Writing demands that a scribbler be old-fogeyish enough to force living into coherence. To write is to be a traditionalist, and although I think the marginalia of my days akin to illustrations in ancient books, they are not the same. Nevertheless, much of the marginalia which I encounter now and which appeals to me occurs in books. The books are not six hundred years old. For the most part they were published at the end of the nineteenth and the beginning of the twentieth century. All are used and soiled. Many hands have held and battered them in the process, endowing them with life. New volumes are sterile, whey-faced, their pages crisp and glaring. Their owners didn't play baseball in high school and strike out seven times in a row. No one ever called them Cuddles, and the books appear untouched by life. They aren't liverish and speckled with lesions. Their spines are firm and straight. Humanizing Time hasn't broken them and ripped their covers into scabs.

The hard covers of old books are often canvases for marginalia. Last week I read *Cosey Corner* published in 1901 and written by Elizabeth Thomasina Meade Smith. L. T. Meade wrote some 300 books, many novels for and about girls. Neither Meade nor her writings are well-known library names. Although the two really have little in common, I associate anonymity with humility, not with ineptness, certainly not in the case of Meade whose books—despite being lukewarm pot boilers—often delight and entertain. They are also cheap. Used bookstores sell early editions from three to six dollars. The prices do not transform the volumes into expensive artifacts. Instead, the modest prices allow readers to relax, almost inviting people to use them as temporary coasters and not be concerned if they spill chocolate or Coca-Cola on them, in short to mark them and record their presence without worrying.

The subtitle of *Cosey Corner* was "How They Kept a Farm." The book's cover was almost iconographic depicting a quiet yet active agrarian idyll. In the front of the illustration, a girl sat on the top rail of a fence, her feet resting on a stile and steadying her. Her hair was blond and sunny. She wore a baggy smock dress rumpled by use and washing. Clumped over her head and looking like a bucket turned upside down was a sunhat. Behind her rose a cottage with a red roof and two front windows, each with six panes. In front of the cottage, a countrywoman supervised a man digging. Also on the cover were four trees with white trunks and black limbs. Across the ground stretched a rug of green grass. In places the rug was threadbare, the green worn away, not by feet, but by the hands of readers. On the spine of the book a rooster stood upright guarding a hen as she bent over pecking the ground. The story was sentimental and sweet. While they tried to earn money to pay a debt incurred by co-signing a bill for a friend who subsequently went bankrupt, the parents of four children sent their offspring to board with old friends. The Burgins owned Honeysuckle Farm and were a kindly childless couple who tended to the children much as the rooster protected the hen.

I read the book more for marginalia than the narrative. How nice to recognize the parlor in the farmhouse. In the middle of the table, glass cases covered wax flowers. On the wall hung prints from the *Graphic* and the *Illustrated London News*. Somewhere in my mind dozed memories of wax fruit as well as flowers and of prints, these last usually Currier and Ives, one depicting a curly-haired little girl holding a rag doll, in others, horses, either racing or pulling a sleigh over a snow-covered road curving around a fence enclosing a Christmas farmhouse. After entering the parlor, an experienced reader will know that Burgins once had a child named Polly. "Wee Polly" died when she was young. She "is better off and I have ceased to murmur at the will of God," said Mrs. Burgin, or Roly-Poly, as her husband called her.

The children were responsible and entrepreneurial. They wanted to pay their way and not be a burden on their distant parents. With the Burgins' help and quiet supervision, they moved into Cozy Corner, a small cottage on the farm. There they grew vegetables, picked blueberries, tended bees, and sold tea to passersby. Like Vicki's and my flat in the Mansfield Apartments, Cozy Corner had "a dear little kitchen," a tiny sitting room, and two bedrooms—more than enough space for happiness. Among other gifts, Mr. Burgin gave the children Clover, "the sweetest calf that has ever come into the world." In the middle of Clover's forehead was a white star that "gleamed like snow in summer." Clover's appearance was unique, at least to me. I have never seen snow in summer, yes, ice during a hailstorm, but it melted quickly and didn't gleam. The children weren't perfect. Occasionally their grammar wandered astray. When urged to work harder shelling peas, Arthur responded, "I am sure I are helping." Most events in the novel were gentle and so pastoral they seemed other-worldly. Once or twice, however, a jagged remark pierced the bucolic fabric. The fewer questions you ask, a gipsy girl said to the two younger children, "the fewer lies you'll be told."

Inside the back cover appeared an elegant bit of marginalia spoiled by busy insensitivity. Written in cursive and curling like a smooth black stream, its surface silken and broken only by a downbeat was: "To Hilda Thompson with best wishes for her birthday, November 25th 1901 from Herman & Johannes Gerharty. Bradford." Obscuring the inscription was a blue circular library stamp. The stamp was the size of the bottom of a quart milk bottle. Printed around the lip of the circle was "Wilbur L. Cross Library, University of Connecticut." In the center appear a big C, its horns pinching a smaller W. After *Cosey*

Corner, I bought Captain F. S. Brereton's novel *John Bargreave's Gold* from a used book dealer for eight dollars. Published in 1910, the volume was a boy's own adventure, the plot vacillating between hyper and hypotension, the prose sometimes ornately descriptive and to a boy alluring, at other times left-handed and all thumbs. I purchased the book because of marginalia: its title and cover. On the cover an African-American poled a canoe across a stagnant lagoon. At his feet a young blond man leaned against the gunwales firing a rifle at Indians across the lagoon. Behind the Indians rose the forbidding and unexplored jungle of the Mosquito Coast. While one Indian held an ancient muzzle loader, the others shot poisoned arrows at the men in the canoe. The arrows flew across the cover, and when they splashed into the water near the canoe, they looked like daylilies pushing through the ground in late spring. The shafts of the arrows resembled stems of the flowers. While the fletchings near the nock looked like breaking buds, the streams of water thrust into the air by the arrowheads waved like leaves.

Details of the story drifted "into the misty gap between memory and imagining," as Susan Cooper put it in *The Dark Is Rising*. For me the gap was a childhood place, the illustrated margin of my life beyond school, a place fabulously rich with treasure hunts and heathen half-naked days, the war paint on my skin drawn from cuts on my arms and legs. In *The Dark* a line from the "Book of Gramayre" sent Will, the main character of the novel "soaring suddenly aloft as if winged." Unlike "Gramayre," *John Bargreave's Gold* wasn't magical. It was marred by imperialism and cartoonish racism; yet, although the jungle was the site of murders, ravenous alligators, and evenings foggy with clouds of deadly mosquitos, at times it seemed "a fairy glen," a place Brereton wrote, "which mayhap hardly a white man had ever reached before." Maybe, in Brereton's turn of the nineteenth century, white men did not know much about the deep jungle of Mosquitia but untold numbers of boys knew and continue to know it well, having joyously become lost amid its giant trees and in countless places just as foreboding, traveling aloft on wings fashioned from their imaginations.

As I read *Gold*, my memory strayed beyond the truth into seams of marginalia colorful with fantastic recollections of things not done or imagined. Did I once cover my chest and stomach with dizzying lines of white house paint? If I didn't, I should have. Did black vultures surfing low over a dank glade lead me to the body of a malefactor? No, the birds were turkey buzzards and led me to a litter of drowned puppies. In my next childhood, I will follow the Honduran Indian recipe for making poison for arrowheads. First, the adventuresome young brew-master must explore the jungle and find a hard exposed rock. With him he should carry a forked stick and a "vessel of earth." He must be ready when venomous snakes crawl out from the damp underbrush to bask atop the rock. A skillful "cook" should catch ten, dump them into the vessel, and "leave them till they have bitten one another and fought till they are dead." Afterward he should seal the vessel and place it in the hot sun and sand on a riverbank. He must allow the bodies of the snakes to molder which, like the yeast used in making bourbon, causes the mixture to ferment, becoming the stuff of final intoxications. Once the arrowheads have been dipped into the brew then one is ready to hunt down, as one of Brereton's characters put it, a "dog gone murderer."

Besides awakening memories and the imagination and being practical guides to dispatching villains, marginalia diverted readers from the clamorous moment. Many hands had held *John Bargreave's Gold.* The cover was scuffed and grimy with sebaceous oils, and the free endpaper and initial pages of the book had broken from the inner hinge and headband—indications of use that decreased the value of the book to bibliophiles but increased the attraction to me, illustrating that the volume's dry pages once lived and might live again. Inside *Gold* was a bookmark, a page torn from the advertising appendix of another book. Filling both the front and back of the page were statements praising Kathleen Lion's *The Ghost Moth*, "One of the Most Discussed Novels of the Year." In the *Saturday Review*, Gerald Gould commended the novel's "poetical sincerity." "A book showing personality, character, and the charm of intellectual and artistic balance," Philip Tomlinson judged in *Cassell's Weekly*. "Its originality is beyond any doubt," a reviewer declared in *The Observer*. "We shall look forward to the next book." *The Ghost Moth* was published in 1923, and despite the anticipation of the reviewer in *The Observer*, it was the first and last of Lion's novels.

Marginalia are often parts of stories. *The Ghost Moth* was an ending. It didn't lead to other books and vanished after fluttering around the lamp on my desk for a moment. More often, marginalia are beginnings. Was Dorothy Halliburton who wrote her name inside the cover of *Rebel of the School* (1902) a shy, repressed child who dreamed of becoming another, more lively person, someone not afraid to kick up her heels, a girl strong enough to resist bullying and overcome the intimidations of place? Dorothy lived in Akron. Did she ever think herself a sleeping unrecognized beauty? Did she imagine going to bed atop twenty mattresses and twenty feather-beds and not being able to sleep because a queen had hidden three small peas on the bottom of the bedstead?

Josh says the Republican members of the Tennessee legislature are too stupid to pound sand. They are the dubs "you see in groceries asking butchers how to tell if a chicken is ripe." In hope of understanding the legislators better, I bought *Sunbeams*, a book almost overripe with "Humor, Sarcasm, and Sense" written in 1900 by the author of *Peck's Bad Boy*. The book was helpful. It made me realize that Josh was sapient. The legislators were imbeciles, people who'd never be able to distinguish between dog meat and goat meat sausages, even if the former were seasoned with woofs and curly tails and the latter with "hoofs" and bleats. I purchased *Sunbeams* from Walk A Crooked Mile Books in Williamsburg, Pennsylvania. Amid the humor and sense, I found a bookmark, not a Beginning or an End, but a Middle, one that cast a quick shadow over the sunbeams. In blue ink in a rounded schoolgirl script on a three by four-and-a-half-inch page torn from a notepad advertising "Heublein Arrow Liquors" in Hartford were lines from a song first recorded half a century ago: "whoever finds this I love you, whoever finds this, I need you. I don't even have anyone to talk to so whoever finds this, I love you." "A seventh-grader fantasizing being old enough to be lovesick and scribbling down a bit of her favorite song," Vicki said. "Yes, I know," I said, "but a lot of people young and old don't have many friends. Last week a widow told me that she took yoga classes at the community center to talk to people. 'After I go home, the only voices I hear come from the television.'"

The next day the oldest man in the locker room sighed then said, "I feel embalmed, and I envy friends who have gotten the Big It over and no longer must sit down to put on trousers."

Later that morning I had my teeth cleaned. Atop a table in the waiting room practically commanding attention stood a cardboard sign: "SNORING and unsure of your options? Ask your dental hygienist or dentist today!" "There are oral appliances that are highly effective at eliminating or minimizing the problem," the sign continued reassuringly. "I couldn't find a registration sheet for Snorers Anonymous," a man sitting in an armchair said to me. "I asked the receptionist if she had the sheet, but she shook her head and told me to talk to the dentist." That afternoon four of us old bookmen, maybe the last of that mongrelly breed hereabouts, met in the library to drink coffee and toast our friend Kent's 93rd birthday. We scrutinized fading marginalia: gossip about dead scribblers and anecdotes from forgotten novels. Albeit wormy, the cherry on our chat was an ancient joke Kent told. A Nebraska witticism from his boyhood, Kent said. "What's worse than ants in your pants?" he asked. When the four of us looked puzzled, Kent said "uncles," and we burst into laughter, hearty and because of the unsmiling social moment in which we are malingering maybe a little chagrined.

Do inscriptions and bookmarks in forgotten novels matter? They do to readers for whom marginalia constitutes life—sapient readers attuned to small matters, that is, to ways of the world. One of the first books I wrote is being translated into Farsi. I have long hankered to visit Iran. "The book gives me an excuse to visit," I wrote my son Edward. "Please don't go," Edward replied. "I feel much the same as I did about your working as a bagger in Price Chopper [an idea I entertained ten years ago to make retirement interesting]. Because of your outspokenness, a trip to Iran would not end well for you." "Instead," Edward suggested, "write a travel essay describing a journey to Iran. Make it up like you do most things you write. Fill the essay with Iranian characters met along the way. Don't give away the game—that the trip is fictive—at the outset or even at all. Make it a journey you took in your younger days, not later than 1970. Remember the old saw that bad people make good stories and bad neighbors, and good people make good neighbors and bad stories." "Crib from travelogues written more than eighty years ago," he continued. He also suggested I entitle the essay "My Friend the Ayatollah" and travel with a clerical confidant who could be a font of wise sayings, maxims, and non-sequiturs, statements like, "Sam, Alexander had Bucephalus and Mohammed the donkey Ya'fur. Get yourself a woman.—Do not be a gray man. The devout are brightly colored. Those who die for the faith are the brightest of all.—I have studied your nation's history. They say that Abraham Lincoln was honest. But I have looked into his soul, and he was a Moslem.—The best fatwas stick like dung on the haunches of a camel crossing the Dasht-e-Kavir in summer.—A Soviet car is worthless even for parts. Still, perhaps Lenin had a point," and "The most deserving of charity are those who ask. Initiative should be rewarded, even in beggars." Decades ago, I'd have followed Edward's suggestion. Then my verbs were active, and it didn't take much to convince them to heist up their dresses, kick off their high heels, and shout "Wahoo." Now they are intransitive, and on their best sentence days, they bolt pills and stutter about on walkers rarely lusting after predicates.

Escaping the truths of one's years and devoting one's days to covers, fly leaves, and end sheets are very appealing. I especially like knowing it is harder for bulldozers to destroy fictions than apartments. I have begun organizing my journey. I will travel first-class on an Omani camel. Hashem my companion will accompany me on a Hassawi donkey. A Saker falcon will perch on my right shoulder. Nowadays falconry doesn't interest me, but sixty years ago I was a different fellow, "a real highflier," the American consul in Muscat may have said. Few people would believe.... Anyway, Hashem and I will travel north from Bandar-e-Abbas and work our way into the Lut Desert. We intend to leave Storrs and the present as soon as I finish Meade's *Daddy's Girl* (1900). I didn't plan to read the book, but the initial paragraph seduced me. "Philip Ogilvie and his pretty wife were quarrelling, as their custom was, in the drawing room of the great house in Belgrave Square, but the Angel in the nursery knew nothing at all about that." The Angel's mother was, in the crass vernacular of the present, a dreadful bitch, a selfish spendthrift who loved money not people. The Angel was beguiling, a sugary tomboy who wondered "if Jesus Christ thinks me pretty." Her father was too decent for this world and urged her to "make goodness the first thing in life." Her nurse was sensibly outspoken and warned her that if she drank wine as a child she would "grow up to be drunk as a hog."

Written on the titlepage of my copy was the inscription "Nettie from Ida T. 1908." If the Lut were more hospitable to little girls, especially those at least a hundred and twenty years old, I'd invite Nettie to accompany Hashem and me. We'd eat bread dipped in olive oil and za'atar, and maybe she'd smack her lips and say "golloptious." Time educates the palate. Because Nettie was a conventional English schoolgirl, she probably wouldn't immediately appreciate many Iranian dishes, among them my favorite delicacy: the heads of dormice, their cheeks stuffed with dates seasoned with thimbles of Arak and dustings of powdered Egyptian canopic worms, the whole baked until the skulls become the toothsome texture of crackling. I suspect she'd also be slow to munch Hashem's campfire delight, spiny-tailed lizard, roasted and basted with leben rich with cumin and turmeric. More to Nettie's taste would be Meade's books, and I'd be sure to take two or three of her tales with me, say *Bashful Fifteen* and *Polly a New-Fashioned Girl.* Every night I'd kiss Nettie like Daddy kissed his Angel. Afterward I'd read to her until both of us fell asleep.

8

Through the Summer in Eighty Days

Vicki's and my eighty days weren't quite so lively as those Jules Verne's Phileas Fogg spent circumnavigating the globe. Moreover, we were each other's Passepartout and didn't go to Calcutta or Yokohama. From our house in Beaver River, we only went south twelve miles through Port Maitland and Hebron to Yarmouth and five miles north along the Gulf of Maine to Salmon River. We travelled in a four-year-old Subaru and didn't board any steamers or trains. Sometimes we stopped for road repairs, but never did a herd of bison or a gang of Sioux disrupt our progress. At our destinations we drank coffee and shared breakfast and club sandwiches. Once or twice, we split slices of coconut cream pie and a bacon-burger oozing "the works," but never did we season our moods with hashish. Generally, we went to the same places, forty-four times to D. J.'s Store and Diner in Salmon River and twenty-five times to Tim Hortons on the site of the old railway station in Yarmouth. On the latter trips we meandered a bit, going to the town library, Canadian Tire, and the grocery at Walmart. Occasionally our travels exhausted us, and we strayed and ate meals outside our usual destinations, at the food counter at Sobey's grocery or The Dinner Plate where until I realized I was 81 and Vicki 71, I thought we were the only people under seventy. At the Plate

I ate fried clams twice. In fact, I ate clams seven times during the summer, all fried except once in a chowder at D. J.'s.

A twenty-thousand-pound wager spurred Fogg's travels. During the summer, Vicki and I spent twenty-thousand dollars on, among other things, travel, taxes, and house repairs. Although not quite equal to Fogg's wager, our twenty was a hefty amount for us. In truth matters don't have to be exact. There is an elegance, a well-bred insouciance, in approximation. Our summer wanderings occurred 151 years after Verne's novel began to appear in France. *One* is a matter of little importance, and for the page our summer took place a celebratory 150 years after the English publication of *Around the World in Eighty Days*. Additionally, we spent 81 rather than 80 days travelling the summer. Although 80 is rounded and tastefully balanced, 81 is better, not only my age but also the product of nine times nine, an iconographic number, in our part of Nova Scotia bearing religious significance. The only mail Vicki and I received during the summer was *The Clare Shopper*, an advertising paper published every fortnight. Amid ads for firewood, used backhoes, and notices announcing meetings of pregnancy and prostate support groups appeared St. Jude's Novena.

> May the sacred heart of Jesus be adored, loved and preserved through the world, now and forever. Sacred Heart of Jesus pray for us. St. Jude, worker of miracles, pray for us. St. Jude, hope of the hopeless, pray for us. Say this prayer 9 times a day for 9 days. By the 8th day your prayer will be answered. It has never been known to fail. Publication must be promised. Thank you. St. Jude.

Every issue of the *Shopper* contained two or three notes thanking St. Jude. For my part, I don't know what the 81 days did or did not do for me. Matters of cause and effect are generally mysterious. In any case as Isaac Watts put it in "Our God, Our Help in Ages Past," "Time like an ever-rolling stream, / Bears all its sons away; / They fly forgotten, as a dream / Dies at the opening day."

I did not plan shadowing Phileas Fogg and traipsing through eighty days. I imagined spending the summer in Connecticut puttering around on the page and in the house. In fact, on learning I was going to Canada, Edward wrote Vicki. "Be careful with Dad," he urged, "he is old and worn out." Worn, but not completely out—nevertheless forty years ago days breezed by, causing me to regret the approach of October. In contrast this past summer dragged like an endless Alexandrine. We did not have television or the Internet or email. Regular mail was not forwarded from Connecticut, and the telephone was broken. Iron made the water undrinkable and except for the warmth put out by the small wood-burning cook stove in the kitchen, the house was unheated. I'd lived with the absences for decades, but now instead of freeing me from distracting minutiae, the emptiness weighed me down, and, to use Vicki's phrase, I experienced "The Forlorns." Reclusiveness became a burden, and simplicity lost its allure. "Less weight equals more encounters," Paolo Rumiz wrote. For the old less weight often increases solitude and decreases encounters. As things vanish, so do the memories associated with them and the stories that rise out of their presence. By summer's end, I occasionally imagined I resembled one of the black spruce in the sphagnum wood behind the blueberry field. The trees' roots were shallow and arthritic, palsied, loosening their grasp of the ground, making them susceptible to bacterial winds, causing them to totter and lean like me. Many of their branches were broken; their pith, waterlogged, the collars cuffing them to the trunk, frayed and undone. Mottled with green and black lichens, their bark looked warty with keratoses and scabs. Horsehair lichens hung from their limbs ragged like the tails of ponies that had raced through brush snarly with burdock and thorns.

Such thoughts were accurate, but they were also evanescent. One morning Vicki warned me that if I didn't exercise more, I'd become an invalid. That afternoon as I walked down the lane toward the drumlin overlooking the Gulf of Maine, gloom seemed to emanate from the wood. But then suddenly my mood lightened, unaccountably as moods do throughout people's lives. I remembered a letter I received before leaving Storrs. "I'll never forget," a friend wrote, "a Belle Meade Club matron saying at one of your book signings in Nashville. 'I've known Sammy since he was a little boy. He was always turning bugs loose in the house. Poor Katharine.'" "A memory like that wouldn't pop up in Connecticut," my correspondent judged. "No, it wouldn't," I said, smiled, and increasing my pace hurried on to the top of the drumlin. As I stood there, I heard the high piping call of a bald eagle, shrill above the distant wash of the breaking waves, the only time during the summer I heard an eagle. "Weary, but not out yet," I thought. On the way back to the house, I mulled "The Bumblebee Good-Night Story," a tale Vicki suggested I write. Chubby little larva underground, I thought, delighting in dreaming about summer days of lavender and lupine, foxglove and goldenrod.

In Connecticut, I intended to write an essay entitled "Questions and Answers." Before leaving Storrs, I collected several questions, all from books. Unless a question supplied an answer in its asking, I didn't plan to include responses. The questions themselves satisfied me. In George Singleton's *Staff Picks*, Uncle Cush said to his nephew Drum, "All lawn mowers run on gas. After I eat pinto beans, I get gas. What does that say about me?" Sometimes a statement made me wonder about Vicki's and my life, not about the dietary effects of Phaseolus vulgaris, but about the activities we imposed upon our canine housemates. On weekdays Vicki walks the dogs on campus, and we assume not only are the strolls beneficial but also that the dogs relish them. Instead, perhaps, the walks are a nuisance, and the dogs would prefer dozing under the kitchen table dreaming about the Rabbit of the Baskervilles. An aged friend of Margery Sharp's *Cluny Brown* walked his pet tortoise in Kensington Gardens. He confided to Cluny that he wasn't sure if the tortoise enjoyed the outings, "whether it didn't after all think, 'Damn the grass.'"

Most questions concerned the everyday, the way people who owned Craftsman lawn mowers and bought groceries at Price Chopper lived. They reflected on muted, decaffeinated, blood pressure lowering activities. "Domenica Macdonald, anthropologist, resident of Edinburgh, observer of humanity and believer in the old-fashioned and increasingly rare virtue of tolerance," Alexander McCall Smith recounted in *The Enigma of Garlic*, "looked out her window onto the cobbled street below and wondered what to cook for dinner." It wasn't a "question on which she would spend much time—nor was it one with which she engaged emotionally." Yet it was a subject people ponder almost daily. "Do you think?" I asked Vicki last night, "that readers will be intrigued by our going to Big Y yesterday and getting a Covid booster and while waiting for the pharmacist meeting a woman named Diana after Paul Anka's song?" "No," Vicki said. "Well, how about the fact that mine was the

51st shot Amanda gave yesterday?" "No," Vicki repeated. "Okay, how about yours being Amanda's 52nd shot?" Vicki did not answer.

Some questions I gathered were in verse. In my case Wordsworth's assertion that the child was the father of the man is partly true. Most of the poetic questions involved bugs. My favorite was Oliver Wendell Holmes's "To a Katydid," a poem appropriate to the sound of late summer evenings and the beginning of fall. "Oh tell me where did Katy live, / And what did Katy do? / And was she very fair and young, / And yet so wicked, too?" the poem began. For a while I considered compiling a signature of insect verse, but at the start of itching and scratching season Vicki and I left Connecticut. Initially the eighty days seemed a refrain echoing past summers. As usual we took *The Cat* ferry to Yarmouth. We arrived at the dock in Bar Harbor early and walked Jack and Mee, the dogs, on the campus of the College of the Atlantic. The college was modest and friendly. "It doesn't mold undergraduates into fans, and branding doesn't undermine appreciation of place," I said to Vicki. "You said that last year," Vicki responded.

Each year despite our owning property, paying taxes, and appearing in July, customs shunts us to the side and rips through our car. Villainous gang-banging tourists pass through with a smile and good wishes. "You look suspicious," we were told last year. We are always tired having gotten up at two in the morning to catch the ferry. But suspicious—a clean-shaven octogenarian dressed like an advertisement from an L.L.Bean catalogue and driving a four-year-old Subaru without tinted windows, not an illegal immigrant, no skulls or snakes tattooed on his neck or arms, clearly not transporting drugs, alcohol, or guns, instead carrying two partially blind sixteen-year-old rescue dogs, not Rottweilers or Dobermans but Chihuahuas? "Show me the deed to your property," an official demanded this year. "That's not required. Consult your computer record and you'll see we've come here since the 1940s." "It makes my day," another official boasted, "to send someone back." "Petty, Stalinist clerks," another summer resident said.

After rummaging through our suitcases in the parking lot and finding nothing illegal, a coarse official rooted under the seats. Since 1956 I have kept the shell of a box turtle, terrapene carolina, under the front seat of every car I've owned. It is a good luck charm. I found it beside a railway track in Hanover, Virginia. The drag from a passing train flipped the turtle and killed it. When I was a boy, I saved so many turtles from roads and track beds that the meringue of football and baseball, senior class vote-getter, and all the this's and that's introduced by "Most" which appeared beneath my picture in my high school yearbook should have been erased. In their place "The Box Turtle's Best Friend" ought to have been inscribed in bold Old English type. Thinking he'd discovered contraband, the official took the shell and disappeared into an office. Twenty-five minutes later he returned and announced the box turtle was an endangered species. The Indian star tortoise is threatened, and the African spurred tortoise is endangered. While the latter lives in the Sahel and can weigh two hundred pounds, the carapace of the former rises into distinct lumps from which rays radiate like sunshine. Neither turtle resembles the small Carolina terrapin. "I can fine you three hundred thousand dollars for having this, but I am going to let you go this time," the man said, handing me my shell and not having the sense to admit he'd behaved foolishly. "No, you can't," I mumbled, adding the word *you* followed by a fitting epithet, a word commonly used by sewer workers on the job. For several days thereafter when customs came to mind, I muttered phrases, referring to the man's family bramble.

One night I imagined a traveler arriving in Yarmouth with a lucky black cat bone mounted on the dashboard of his car, just the sort of item to attract the attention of the customs official. Taking a person's lucky bone brings disaster. If the official confiscated the bone, his days, the few left him, would be bleak with misfortune. Good anecdotes are balms bringing forgetfulness. One morning in Tim Hortons after I mentioned my experience in Yarmouth, John recounted crossing from Ontario to the United States to visit his daughter in Indiana. Accompanying him were his two sons. John had been a man about town, and his three children had different mothers. "Going to visit your daughter?" the customs man at the American border exclaimed. "No, you are on the way to appear on *The Jerry Springer Show*."

In *The Private Life of Spies* Alexander McCall Smith wrote, "Sooner or later, the place where you are destined to be will come and claim you. It always does. You may think you've escaped, but you never have: like gravity, such places pull you back, assert their control of your life." Life is repetitive. One day leads to the next; one season to another, and in Vicki's and my case, one summer in Nova Scotia to the following summer. Habit becomes so ingrained that a person's actions seem destined. Come June Canada claims us, and the summers repeat themselves like refrains. Some years the refrain is weaker, but paradoxically its pull may be stronger. This is especially true for the elderly, whom continuance reassures as their lives become increasingly fragile. That's the reason they react strongly to bulldozer-and-dynamite development, thinking it not simply ruinous but a personal affront, an attack undermining sensible, accustomed ways of living. The physical landscape is but one among many landscapes inhabited by, and because of familiarity, valued by oldsters. Language is another. As a result, octogenarians often strongly condemn changes in grammar, for example, the "idiosyncratic" use of preferred pronouns. Moreover, rarely do the old react without an inelegant exclamatory phrase to erasing or changing the name of a holiday long on the calendar, for example, rebranding Columbus Day, labelling it Indigenous People's Day.

After Vicki and I landed in Yarmouth, our lives slipped into familiar routines. Every morning, I split logs in the barn then built fires in the kitchen stove. Because her bed sags badly, years ago Vicki named it The Bucket. Before getting into bed at night, she always sang a sea shanty, not something she has ever done on a flat mattress in landlocked Storrs. Within a week of my arrival, I usually injure myself. When I was a boy, I was measled with scabs, and like roads drawn on a map, cuts sliced across my skin in lines. Most were country lanes, but occasionally, particularly if I were having a good rambunctious time, a superhighway. As could have been predicted, summers in Nova Scotia weren't bruiseless. In the past I caught my foot climbing to the loft in the barn and falling backward banged down onto the floor. Happily, the wide boards were loose, and they sagged under my weight and caught me like a hammock. Once a stone wall crumbled beneath me and threw me onto a granite boulder. On another occasion, I slipped in loose dirt and rolled part of the way down a bluff overlooking the Bay of Fundy. A hedge of bay and meadowsweet prevented my falling to the beach below.

This year, four days after starting to split wood, I dropped the ax on my left foot. The butt smashed my middle toe knocking the nail akimbo. I went into the kitchen and sitting at the table pulled the nail off with pliers. Because I take thinner, blood ran in rivulets. In truth, the injury was slight. In fact, when Vicki saw the blood, she made an unkinder verbal cut. Two weeks later I fell in the scrub behind our south field. Several winters ago, the area had been lumbered. Skidders trenched the ground. Afterward chest-high ferns and roils of briars obscured leghold traps of shattered limbs and chats. Two summers ago, I also fell. Regaining my feet so exhausted me I determined to avoid the scrub in the future. Sensible reformation is easier for the young than the old. Even though I used two ski poles as canes, levering myself off the ground took three-quarters of an hour. To clear a space, I kicked and rolled on my sides, thrashing back and forth, first on my stomach then on my shoulders. Before I stood, my hands were as thorny as a porcupine's tail. "You must have looked like one of the bugs you admire, on your back wiggling your arms and legs. You poor beetle," Vicki, rather Nurse Victoria, said. I did not return to the scrub, but I wondered what beetle I resembled. A click beetle, I decided, not a carrion beetle. Although every month nowadays I write at least one condolence letter, I hadn't become food for a Nicrophorus, one of my favorite beetles, orange waving across its black elytra looking like bats in flight. Later I changed my mind and thought I looked like a pill bug, roly-poly and domestic, colonizing the damp house during fall and winter, but also fragile, falling prey to spiders who slung webs around baseboards and under bay windows. Pill bugs are wanderers, and some mornings Vicki found one or two in the bathroom who'd slipped off the wall board and tumbled into the tub. When she prodded them with her index finger, they pulled themselves into balls after which she rolled them into her hand, and picking them up, carried them outside and freed them in the lilies beside the porch. Longfellow got things wrong. No one I know lives a sublime life and is so egotistical he imagines grinding footprints into the sands of time. The people I admire rescue pill bugs and spiders, sundry everyday creepers and crawlers, excepting a few outlaws like ticks and lady mosquitoes. When such a person dies, his presence lingers unobtrusively for a moment then quietly vanishes into lost, silent Time.

I escaped what I thought the greatest risk of injury. Bedrooms in the house are upstairs, and to reach them a person climbs "The Himalayas," fourteen steps, each tread nine inches higher than the previous tread. On the left side of the steps is a sturdy banister, a sherpa on whom I leaned going up and down. Our dog Jack was sixteen years old. Throughout previous summers he bounded up the steps and slept in a dog bed in Vicki's and my bedroom. Now he had difficulty walking on level ground. His legs splayed, and often he wobbled and fell to the side. The first night in Four Winds, Jack stood at the foot of the steps looking at me expectantly. I carried him up the stairs in my right arm, locking my left hand on the railing. Jack weighed only eleven pounds, a weight that once I would not have noticed. This year it tired me, and usually on the steps I paused and panted, pulling Jack into my chest so if my arm weakened he wouldn't slip out of my grasp. During the summer Vicki and I carried Jack up the stairs at nine or ten at night then down at two in the morning so he could relieve himself outside. Afterward we carried him back. At seven, I brought him down for the day. That amounted to climbing and descending fifty-six steps with Jack. That, however, was only half the number of steps we carried him. Every time he went outside, I carried him down and up the steps to the porch, just three steps each way but at least eleven times a day for an additional sixty-six steps and a total each day of approximately 122 steps. Twice my right leg buckled and often I staggered, but never did I fall.

In Romain Gary's novel *Lady L.*, when painters praised her style and grace, Lady L. said, "it can all be learned from flowers.... A branch of lilac was a lesson in grace; watching swans gliding proudly on the lake, looking at flowers, she suddenly knew more about poise than all the manuals of comportment." In "Tintern Abbey," Wordsworth wrote that nature was the anchor of his purest thoughts, "the guardian of his heart" and the "soul" of his moral being. In nature he felt a presence that disturbed him with the "joy of elevated thoughts," "a sense sublime," "a motion and a spirit" that impelled all thinking things and all objects of thought and rolled "through all things." How comforting it would be to know that a numinous presence was "interfused" in the rocks and trees, birds and insects, in the grass, in the stars, and in the deep sea. How inspiring to believe that a spirit sowed asters and goldenrod, purple loosestrife, ladies tresses, and queen of the meadow across the ground transforming old fields into freshening stained-grass windows. How uplifting it would be to see the gardening hand of a deity planting wild mint and forget-me-nots in damp ditches and adorning the shoulders of dirt roads with Queen Anne's lace. How heartening to accept that the soul of a moral essence-controlled disorder and linked everything in sacral kinship. Alas, only youth can imagine such an overarching sublimity. Old age cannot. Long living teaches that life, and the world are secular and chaotic and that dreams of a unifying transcendence are self-deluding illusions, often corrupting, dangerous, and paradoxically tribal.

Lady L., not Wordsworth got it right. Following a "sylvan Wye" or meandering down the lane at Four Winds, affects the social person. As Lady L. absorbed comportment from flowers, so trimming around the house and barn imposed structure on my day as well as the grounds. This summer, as in the past, I pulled nooses of Virginia creeper from the roses in the side yard. I cut down bales of smothering Japanese knotweed. I sawed dead limbs out of the willow above the pet cemetery. I pruned the rhododendron and the golden elder. From some of the paths I blazed in the past I cleared adventitious alders and bay, winterberry and blackberry. Because trees had fallen across them, I neglected and abandoned several other paths. Once I would have cleared ways around the trees, but now the task was too onerous.

Every day I walked the lane and wandered into nearby fields. I didn't learn comportment, but I experienced contentment. The blueberry field hadn't been bushwhacked in a year and had grown into scratchy shambles. Not educated by school, or blade, it radiated sensible disorder, a weedy, practically aristocratic, nonchalance in the presence of which concerns about distant happenings disappeared. It taught that events which mattered were local and that small doings were not only the most important things in life but that they constituted life itself. When a sojourner is on the road to the Kingdom, as old-time gospellers phrased it, he ought to realize that the Kingdom is underfoot in the *now* and not in the *future*. In July, blue-eyed grass spread through the field glowing like stars and turning the ground into a sky. The rough stems of knapweed grabbed my shoelaces and forced me to notice the flower heads looking like toy pincushions of purple and silver. In September, bushes of New England asters and veins of goldenrod opened seams in the rugs of flat-topped asters blanketing fields.

The wildflowers begot a secular piety, an appreciation free from distant gods and harrowing doctrines. The plants were only a part of summer's festive landscape: tamaracks graceful as ballerinas, mountain ash bearing salvers of rusty-orange berries, and stands of poplars trembling in the wind, their leaves green then silver. At the corners of fields, aged apple trees slumped and broke, their trunks necklaced by sapsuckers. Here and there an apple grew blotched and tumorous, its taste tart as unwaxed living. Red admiral butterflies puddled on the lane then settled on flat-topped asters, the scarlet ribbons on their wings tying the flowers into small bouquets. Near the ground wood nymphs leaned and blinked through grasses. Repetitions are simultaneously the same and different. The sights I saw I'd seen before. In the silence beyond news and screen, they were always fresh and freshening. Early in the morning dew turned bent grass silver and blue and weighed the stems down, so they leaned over and through one another like spider webs. In the low damp were bulrushes, sword grass, Canadian rush, its flowers in tight dark constellations, and lanky wool grass. At summer's end, the wool grass's flowers became fuzzy bundles loose as rags beside a kitchen sink. Unless dementia has stripped him, no man is an island existing only in the present. The freshening applied to the past as well as the present. When a skunk sprayed a marauding cat in the basement, the fragrance made me recall perfumed boyhood days, exuberant times amid apple and pear trees in fields over the hills and seventy-five years away.

To kill Gorgons, Perseus travelled into the heart of the Unshapen Land where nothing had a name or a place and there was neither night nor day. To slay Medusa, Perseus looked at her reflection in his shield. Looking at something directly enables defining and shaping. It also restricts imagination. Naming determines, and studying and describing an object doesn't turn a person into stone, but it hardens perception. By Perseus's not staring directly at her and seeing only a reflection, Medusa remains in part a shapeshifting imagined being. Knowing that the alcoholic aroma along the lane arose from branches broken from wild raisin did not describe the redolence in clinical detail. But the walker who knew its source probably does not pause and wonder when he notices it. In Herbert Read's *The Green Child*, the mysterious child cannot describe the world from which she came because "there were no earthly words to exchange for her memories." In addressing the child, Olivero, the hero of the book, used words he knew the child had never heard and could not understand. He was forced to used "those words," Read wrote, "because words and things grow together in the mind, grow like a skin over the tender images of things, until words and things cannot be separated."

In the pages of guidebooks are matters that expand life. Yet, that same matter can satisfy and limit. Too often the knowledgeable discover identity and neglect to look beyond definitions. Often, I wanted to wander from the Shapen Land and peel words off of things. In September, mushrooms blossomed, among others, smooth chanterelles curling in yellow waves beside the lane and in a mowed plot atop the bluff, the flaky red and orange caps of fly agaric swelling through the grass. I'd forgotten the names of many familiar mushrooms.

Instead of identifying them, I decided simply to observe their coloration. On one mushroom the cap and gills were ochre and the stem yellow and thready, almost knock-kneed. Another was rainbowed, its cap orange, gills white, and stem pale yellow. I hoped by forgoing concern about identity and simply looking that perhaps I'd think anew. I admired the colors and on a later walk showed the mushrooms to Vicki. But unpeeling names didn't free me to escape declarative clarity and imagine and think differently. I wondered if renaming objects would alter perspective. It did not. I was too old to become limber in body or mind. At times I thought inborn and ingrained instinct determined my view. Was it instinct or education that made tansy ragwort's enameled brightness disturbing or the white of Amanita virosa, destroying angel, so pure I guessed it was impure and poisonous? Dubbing funnel web grass spiders napkin spiders seemed clever, but it did not change the webs that lay shining atop the grass outside the kitchen meadow every damp September morning.

Of course, our woods and fields differ from season-to-season and from year-to-year. The changes influence my thoughts, but rarely do they affect the way I think. Usually, they are confined to the sensory, to the seen or heard. This summer fireweed did not appear in the blueberry field. Blackberries were small and grainy, and a scrub of alders, bay, wild raisin, and cinnamon ferns overflowed into the lane smothering shadbush. Sheep laurel vanished. The scrub was impenetrable and so thick the stone wall running through it disappeared. No longer did I spot short-tailed weasels scampering across the stones and darting into gaps. For that matter I did not see foxes or porcupines, and although I followed deer tracks across fields, the single deer I saw was a doe standing next to the laundromat in Yarmouth looking bored as if she were waiting for a hamper of clothes to dry. Yellow jackets disappeared. When I barracked through overgrowth, no longer did I worry about bumping into or stepping on a hornets' nest. At full moon no great horned owls called from atop the church across the road from our house. Willets were not heard on the beach. Offshore, terns did not sail and swoop, and cormorants did not beat low over the water beyond the breaking tide. Age and the aftereffects of medicines were dampers partly responsible for curtailing my observations. "You've had so much radiation," my friend Josh said before Vicki and I left Connecticut, "that if someone stuck an extension cord in your backside, he could illuminate Hartford for a week." Unsurprisingly, I lacked the energy, and maybe the inclination, to roam not simply the beach and woods as I did in the past but also to explore days themselves.

When I took Jack outside at two in the morning, I didn't remove a chair from the porch and, sitting in the meadow for an hour, study the constellations and count shooting stars. In a glance I recognized Pegasus and Draco. For a moment I wondered if Serpens Cauda shook his tail like a harmless black racer to intimidate stargazers so they would leave him alone, thinking him to be venomous. I didn't bother to look at Hercules. I knew his arms and legs were ludicrously akimbo like those of a pubescent freshman auditioning to be a high school cheerleader. No, after Jack relieved himself, I picked him up, reentered the house, carried him upstairs, and went back to bed.

Still, on a few nights I paused and listened to the tides, the systolic and diastolic beat of water pushing and withdrawing, the rocks high on the beach sometimes clattering, even shrieking, and then on calm moony nights atrial fibrillations, slow and hardly noticeable like my pulse. Upstairs during the day, I often gazed out the bedroom windows, to the southwest over our southern hay field, through the jagged rim of black spruce, then out across the Gulf of Maine, the distant bay at Port Maitland curling like a comforting arm. In the northwest, the Bay of Fundy thrummed around Black Point, swelling then narrowing. Early in the morning, mists drifted white over the khaki bales on our northern hay field, gathering in folds but then eventually sliding over the lower lip of the drumlin ruffling the beach below. Some nights moonlight dappled the tops of waves shaping rungs of silver and golden ladders. Although the vistas did not awaken emotion or provoke thought, they momentarily scrubbed soiling accounts of man's inhumanity from awareness. In doing so, they almost invigorated optimism, the source of the peace that passeth understanding. Almost—nowadays jettisoning chagrin is impossible for anyone not suffering from social encephalitis. "Lynchings by gun," my friend Josh said earlier in the summer, describing a bloody day in Florida or perhaps in Texas, indeed possibly anywhere and everywhere in the United States.

The diminution of birds was the most visible change from the summers of forty years ago. The sky and beach, fields and wood had been plucked. Never did I hear a veery at dusk or a hermit thrush whistle a greeting to morning. Only once did the wild glee of a loon break the silence of an evening. No herons foraged the shallows at Black Point. No robin raced across the side meadow hunting earthworms, looking like it was playing stop-and-go. Only a few sanderlings scooted along the beach in the wake of retreating tides. Even gangs of herring gulls were small and restrained. The waves of chickadees, titmice, and warblers that migrated through the spruce woods and brush bordering fields early every fall had shrunk and flattened. Once upon a time, yellow flickered amid the wood coming and going, blinking, looking like splashings on a Jackson Pollock painting. To be sure the air wasn't barren. But as placid age recalls the passions of youth and wonders what happened to the rain and thunder, the flashes of heat lightning, and the endless sunrises tantalizing with color and sweet possibilities, so I wondered what happened to the birds. Would that I could have spoken to them like St. Francis. For a stranger not old enough to have witnessed the abundance of past years, a banquet remained, a butter tree rich with a merlin slicing past a windbreaker like an arrow, its wings fletchings, a marsh hawk planing low across a hay field, and a kestrel trembling like a floater in the eye then suddenly falling below sight. How nice to lay a fire in the kitchen and be serenaded by a song sparrow, or later, on the porch, rock to the rhythm of a hairy woodpecker drumming a dead birch.

Certainly, I missed other creatures, only glimpsing damselflies and mature caterpillars. Still, there were sights, a hatching of tiny whiskered tussock moth caterpillars banqueting on winterberry and a springtime darner sunning itself on the end of my walking stick. Although the number and variety of birds decreased, there were unexpected additions. At noon one day a murmuration of starlings landed in the side meadow. One summer a pair of starlings nested in the barn, but a numberless flock had never appeared. During one afternoon two bluebirds just beyond fledgling adolescence fluttered about the stubby remnant of a rotted limb for two hours. I hadn't seen a bluebird in the yard before. I'd heard mourning doves in the past but this summer four became residents as did a catbird whose mewing I recognized but thought I'd misheard because I hadn't spotted a catbird at Four Winds previously.

Every summer I read shelves of books. As I wander field and wood without a plan, so I meander scrubs of pages glancing at life. "Through the binoculars of books," Vicki says, "often through the wrong end." I thought about birds frequently. Indeed, the first book I read was *To See Every Bird on Earth* by Dan Koeppel. When I entered the Yarmouth Library three days after arriving in Nova Scotia, Susan greeted me. "This will interest you," she said handing me Koeppel's account of *A Father, A Son, and A Lifelong Obsession*, this last being a study of bird listers. The book began on an island in the Rio Negro River with a group of listers toasting Koeppel's father on his seeing his 7,000th species, the Amazonian black tyrant, a small flycatcher. For many listers, the number of birds mattered more than the birds themselves, more than the birds' surroundings, often more than all the listers' non-numerical experiences. On being diagnosed with cancer and given six months to live, one famous lister decided to forgo immediate treatment and spend her remaining days adding to her list. Seventeen years later as her list neared 8,500 birds, she died in Madagascar in a car wreck. Because the wedding of her daughter coincided with a planned birding trip, she skipped the wedding.

Often books are long topic sentences leading readers to ponder the paragraphs of their lives. All people are listers. Lists may be skeleton keys to identity, if, of course, identity ever hardens and loses fluidity. Few people devote themselves to one list but are instead serial listers, the subjects changing with time and circumstance. In elementary school I listed baseball cards I owned and the books I read. I recorded oddities, for example, one summer the ears of corn eaten at meals. The record for a single sitting was thirteen set at my grandmother's dinner table in Hanover, Virginia. Later I listed the operas and ballets I attended, even later the countries I visited. Afterward when I was child bound, I kept track of the road races I ran. Eventually I threw all those lists away. Academics like me frequently lead closeted lives. In the view of others, and often themselves, they become their CV's or curriculum vitae, that is, the list of the books and articles they wrote, and the awards, and fellowships they won. For too many teachers the lists of speeches made and committees on which they served ooze down pages and through years like psoriasis, ending, if they end, when the sufferers abandon their offices and retire. Then such lists become meaningless and make a person question how he spent his life. Of course, escaping lists is impossible. Rarely does Vicki pay cash for anything. Instead, she uses a credit card, and each month the bank mails her a list of her charges, an accounting she studies carefully. Whenever I visit a physician, a receptionist requests a list of my medications. Recognizing the footprints of deer, raccoon, and hare in Beaver River pleases me. So does noticing a mouse scamper under a dresser and then becoming a little game hunter opening a drawer and beneath a pile of forgotten wool sweaters discovering the weightless remnants of last year's nest, all urine dried, the droppings crumbled and winnowed. But I don't like tracking pills, and I am slightly proud, and simultaneously ashamed of being proud, when I tell the receptionist, "I don't keep a list."

Four Winds is one hundred and sixty years old. Moldings have broken loose and dangle from ceilings. The foundation is crumbling. The roof leaks. A hoarfrost of cold seeps through the bedrooms. The attic belongs to red squirrels. Mold infests walls, and beetles, the floors. The ideal setting for the next season of *Walking Dead*, I thought when we opened the house in July. Vicki and I are old people with things. We have aged beyond the acquisitive into the disquisitive stage of life. Unfortunately, our children are scattered. Francis lives in Connecticut, but Eliza is in California and Edward, in South Carolina. Their lives are modest. Moreover, their needs and tastes differ from ours. Even if they could afford to remove a van crammed with things from Vicki's and my lives, and attic, they wouldn't and shouldn't. The items would burden and smother, not enhance. Four Winds is the heaviest and most worrisome thing weighing Vicki and me down. Vicki cannot bear contemplating selling the property. She has spent almost every summer there since she was born in 1953 and associates Four Winds with happy familial days. Moreover, the property would not sell, and only a person with a pocket deeper than a black hole could accept it as a gift. As a result, each year we manage small chores, "our financial flu shots," Vicki says. Instead of fretting about the outlay, I shrug and divert myself with numbers.

Nothing had been done to the septic system for at least six decades. Convinced that the septic tank was near collapsing and that water would gush out of the bathtub, flow beneath the door, and sweeping down the hall puddle in rank pools in the parlors, Vicki decided to have a plumber inspect the tank. Would that she had engaged Cluny Brown's uncle Mr. Porritt, "a successful plumber." Because he would have billed us at 1944 rates, the year he appeared in Margery Sharp's novel, his charges would have been less than those of the man Vicki hired. But, since Mr. Porritt lived at 15 String Street in Paddington, the expense of a round-trip ticket from London to Halifax would have multiplied our expenditures, not to mention forcing us to endure the inconvenience of fetching him from and returning him to the airport. As it transpired, the cost of replacing the tank amounted to $7,650 and change, the "and change" being an expression tossed off by the affluent with the same aplomb as they carelessly fling C-notes into the breeze. Included in the amount were expenses for dirt and sod, grass seed, and two boys who spread the seed and curried the sod. The HST or Harmonized Sales Tax is 15% in Nova Scotia. On our bill the tax was responsible for $1,147.50 of the charges.

For my kind of lister, that is, a person entranced by numbers, the tax was less a matter of wallet than playpen. Numbers lend themselves to the realistic. Not even the steel wool of words can scrub the grit of life off calculations. I am a summertime outdoorsman. For twenty consecutive summers I bathed rarely. Not once during those many months did I use the indoor water closet. Time has changed me, and I am not quite the woodsman I once was. Still, during this year's eighty-one days in Canada, never did I micturate inside the house. However, the other aperient matter seduced me into calculating. My figures are suspect, and a doctoral graduate of MIT or perhaps a professor at the Wharton School of Business could tinker with them and increase their reliability. However, slavish honesty is boring. All writers, true believers, compassionate neighbors, and loving mates and parents forever distort. Rigorous truth tellers shouldn't be avoided like the plague. They are the plague. On her deathbed the mother of Josephine Humphreys asked her daughter "to find the Book of Truth." On her daughter's assuring her that she'd find it, Humphreys's mother raised her voice and said, "Find it—*and destroy it.*"

In my figures, I did not include washing dishes, the number of times micturition caused someone to flush the toilet, or baths, in Vicki's case a significant figure because she bathed every day. For my part I bathed only eleven times during the summer or once every 7.4 days. My legs have lost the ability to push. If I had stretched out in the tub, I'd still be there. Instead, I sat on a stool, doused my hide with soap, and sprayed water over myself. I got partially clean, but for most of the summer I was a dirty old man. No, I limited my calculations to the cost of using the toilet for disposing of egesta. Vicki and I were in the house for eighty-one days. Vicki's brother Geoff spent two weeks with us. I assumed that our innards functioned normally which led me to conclude that according to my rubric we flushed the toilet 176 times. On the chance that eating an overripe clam or stuffing too many French fries down our gullets may have caused a stomach to perform erratically I tossed in a baker's dozen of flushes bringing the total to 189, each flush thus costing $6.07 in tax. "In Canada there is clearly much to be said for constipation," Josh remarked after I showed him my figures.

Age confines me. As a result, I now roam more by book than in the past when I wandered light-footed, flittering here and there, in Nova Scotia through dank, mossy woods, across grabbing, sucking bogs, and at full moon through the spill of ankle-snapping boulders along the shoreline. This summer I read a book a day. Many were travel books. Phileas Fogg's hurried peregrinations paled beside my armchair jaunts. "I want things to happen," Cluny Brown said, explaining her desire for an eventful life. In travel books almost always one thing generally follows slapdash after another. Rarely does the narrator begin his day with a coffee at Tim Hortons, then after meandering the stacks at the local library spend the afternoon dozing in his car in the parking lot at Walmart while his wife shops inside. Nevertheless, a diet of reading about the faraway frequently seasons a person's perception of the local making the parochial more interesting than chapters of adventuresome bunkum.

Among the first books I read was *Sailing Alone Around the World*, Joshua Slocum's account of circumnavigating the globe. The journey covered forty-six thousand miles, lasted three years, two months, and two days, and was first published serially in *The Century Illustrated Monthly Magazine* in 1899 and 1900. Following Slocum from one port to the next was as tedious as trudging one foot after another through deep snow. For many readers, especially after scores of workaday pages, the familiar is more awakening than the unfamiliar. Only when Slocum landed in Australia did I stop hankering for a corroboree of cyclones to blow him across the Indian Ocean, around the Cape of Good Hope, and northwest up the Atlantic into Newport, the end of his journey. Even so, I ignored his moments in Australia. Instead, I traveled by association to the years Vicki, the children, and I spent there. Perhaps the most successful armchair meandering is that which transports a person into memory. For many people what the public world celebrates as achievements don't matter. Often substance is an illusion raised upon a foundation of branding words.

While I read Frances Mayes's *A Year in the World*, days I spent on Rhodes, Capri, Crete, and Santorini, among other Mediterranean places came to mind. As I read, Jack lay quivering in a bed beside my feet. When I glanced at Jack, I recalled another mongrel shaking at my feet. As I sat in a café on Kos forty years ago, a thin yellow dog darted off a sidewalk and into a road where a car hit him. Afterward, the dog dragged himself off the asphalt. Spine bent and legs trailing, he staggered under my table where he trembled violently then died, his muzzle resting on the vamp of my right shoe.

In Seville, Mayes visited a shop that sold hams. The hams hung from the ceiling. Beneath them sat cups to catch the fat that dripped down their hooves. The skin on one ham, Mayes wrote, looked "like an old saddle." Inside, the meat was the "color of a blood orange." Mayes sampled meat from a black pig then a white pig. Mayes's travels were too rich for the Nova Scotia me. Vicki cooked our meals on a two-burner wood stove in a cold kitchen, and we ate at a swaybacked table, the floorboards under our feet warped and covered with linoleum scuffed gray by three generations of family. Once Mayes's travels might have awakened envy. Now they bored. Oddly, they brought to mind a debutante ball, the girls savories in ribbons and white dresses, the boys tiramisu sweet with the cocoa of black-ties, fresh and not stale, uncalloused by responsibility and corporate living, the evening iced by Lester Lanin and dollops of his soft, soothing music.

Long ago my tastes budded and bloomed. Now, from the perspective of gastronomes, I suppose, they have wilted. The culinary centerpieces of the summer were two evenings Vicki and I drove to the fire hall across from D. J.'s Store in Salmon River. There we played Meat Bingo. All the firemen were volunteers and once a month friends of the department sponsored Meat Bingo fund-raisers. Thirty-eight or thirty-nine people attended. Two-thirds were women, and except for the visiting grandchild, most participants were seventy and over, considerably over. Evenings were inexpensive. A sheet of fifteen games cost five dollars. On each sheet were six games. All six were played at once. When numbers on their sheets were called, players obliterated them with a bingo dabber. Dabbers were six or so inches long and round and looked like hard toothpaste tubes. Colored ink filled them. One end of the tube was soft and spongy and when pressed down on paper left a blot. Devotees kept their dabbers in knitted round carryalls. They also owned an assortment of colors. Each sheet of six games was printed in a different color, red or yellow for example. When playing on a red sheet, the bingo aficionado used a dabber containing red ink, for a yellow sheet, a yellow dabber, blue for blue, green for green, etc. Prizes were modest: a serving of bacon, chicken breasts, or pork chops,

During our second night, I won a Seaquest shrimp ring containing frozen shrimp imported from Vietnam. Unlike the other players who knew each other, Vicki and I were strangers and the only summer residents. We had a good, happy time. People were friendly and concerned, several making sure we knew how to play. The first evening cost $16, ten dollars for two tablets of games, four for two dabbers, and two for a couple of Pepsis. Because we did not purchase new dabbers, the second evening cost four dollars less. Like Mayes, crowds of people have dined at high tables around the world. No one to whom Vicki and I have talked since returning to Connecticut has played Meat Bingo. "Now that," Josh said, "is real cachet." "And their loss," Vicki said adding, "at a certain age, the best happenings are local."

Many travel books follow a tight structure into which the writer inserts events which appear spontaneous but which in fact have been plotted, often to change mood. For example, in one book I read the narrator was in an oncologist's reception room. Hanging on the walls were pastel prints, saccharine depictions of farmhouses, apple orchards, and lazy country streams. While the writer waited to see the doctor, a man entered, registered at the main desk, then after glancing around, said to the receptionist, "Don't you think it would be more appropriate to decorate the room with pictures of graveyards? All the people who come here have cancer." I suspect that the author fabricated the tale as an antidote, hoping that administering it would counteract the somnolent effect of his pedestrian prose. Much as I initially considered writing about questions and sometimes answers, so I noticed narrative oddities—edges, unnecessary parts that jutted out from stories snagging the notice of disinterested readers. In *The Green Child*, a negligible character kept a half dozen cages of hummingbirds in his study. When he opened the cages, the birds buzzed and fluttered around his head. In the room he also had an assortment of quills filled with syrup into which the birds "dipped their tongues." After the birds had lapped their fills and were tired of flying, he eased them back into their cages. Zoological marvels filled the world of the Green Child's birth: three feet long snakes whose scales shined blue and phosphorescent and whose owners draped them around their necks like scarves, and six legged beetles with metallic blue shells which were the size of tortoises and fast as cockroaches. In *Lady L.*, Dicky the Duke of Glendale shared his breakfast with a pet toucan. For the sartorial and social records, Dicky wore a Damascus robe and Turkish slippers, and he and the toucan "enjoyed each other's company." Often a remark stuck out from clogging workaday prose. On the disappearance of a witness to a crime in a mystery, a policeman urged an inspector to search dykes in the neighborhood. Once, he recounted, a woman for whom he was looking fell into a dyke and was too exhausted to haul herself out. "There were eels in the dyke," he added lugubriously to the delight of macabre readers. The conventional inhabitants of an insular community, a narrator noted, would have been shocked "if somebody had observed to them that a sudden death makes a nice change in the daily routine." The remark had little to do with the plot, but the narrator was correct. People beyond a certain age rarely grieve at the disappearance of contemporaries. The deaths don't make them morose. Instead, they enliven living, quickening it with spirited, often gay, frequently fictional, recollections.

Such statements are asides and resemble pieces of a jigsaw puzzle. When placed next to one another, they do not form coherent pictures. What they show is life. Last week I went to a dermatologist. While in the waiting room, a nurse and I discussed family. The woman had six miscarriages after which her doctor said her chances of having a baby "were infinitesimal." One Friday months later the doctor discovered the woman had a tubal pregnancy. The doctor insisted on removing the egg immediately, warning, "It could kill you," "I hesitated," the woman said, "but I promised to return for the procedure Monday after church. The woman was popular in her church. The congregation loved her and knew how much she wanted a baby. In the middle of the service, they formed a circle around her, knelt, and prayed. Each person also gave her a flower from the altar. "I cried and cried," the woman said. That night her lower region felt odd. The next morning when she returned to the doctor to have the egg removed, he discovered it had shifted into her womb. He was flabbergasted. "It was a miracle," she said, "my little boy was a miracle. He is nine years old now, and he's still a miracle."

Age has made me a reader of many parts, not the compliment implied by the phrase, man of many parts. In several novels, stories quickly disappeared, the single trace of reading being a detail, in one book, a character who reversed spelling, baseball becoming llabesab, and Connecticut, Tucitcennoc. I suspect most people have done the same especially when their children were young. They did so not to disguise crudity, but to toy with words, before grammar and spelling books locked them behind rules and purged irreverent playfulness. When Eliza and Francis were in kindergarten, we often addressed them as Azile and Sic Narf. At dinner we reversed classrooms of names, generally breaking down at Otto which spelled backward was Otto, and when turned inside-out was Toot. Vicki and I still occasionally reverse words, "Do you want granola or all bran?" becoming "Od uoy tnaw alonarg ro lla narb?" We don't do it often. Not only are fashioning and deciphering sentences tedious, but our minds are no longer green and pliable. As a result, we are invariably forced to use erasers after two or three words.

The three travel books I most enjoyed were organized around clear narrative lines. In *Headhunters on My Doorstep*, Maarten Troost followed Robert Louis Stevenson's journeys through the South Seas, both men landing at, among other islands, Tahiti, the Marquesas, and Samoa where Stevenson died in 1894. I, too, have followed Stevenson, not by boat but by book, visiting all his novels and most of his nonfiction. Reading Troost did not evoke pictures of cerulean skies and breaking seas, but genial memories. Outside my study window, sharks did not cruise the surf. Instead, cedar waxwings cavorted noisily about the crowns of black spruce. Beyond a stone wall in the morning sun, round bales of hay gleamed, huge doubloons for cattle. They were not the pieces of eight dreamy boys read about in *Treasure Island*, and which led them to spend happy boyhood hours exploring hills and fields hoping to discover Captain Flint's hoard. Still, the bales were enough for me now, bringing to mind Jerseys and Guernseys and hay lofts magical with caves and mysterious tunnels.

In *The Fault Line*, Paolo Rumiz travelled the "Other Europe, From Finland to Ukraine," Mitteleuropa, down from the Hyperborean lands to Odessa. Rumiz's journey took thirty-three exhausting days. He travelled through places where the law was sometimes lawless, places I think I once saw and borders I may have crossed fifty years ago. For octogenarians most reading involves a personal fallacy. "Who was I when I was there?" the old reader asks, closing his book, cocking his head and gazing backward as if seeing something concrete amid the mist of the forgotten and the fictional. In *Between Terror and Tourism: An Overland Journey Across North Africa*, Michael Mewshaw spent three months traveling from Alexandria to Tangier. I lived in Jordan and Syria each for a year. Sand got into my blood, making me a romantic lover of deserts and Damascene lives and moments. At times living in the Mid-East was punishingly and absurdly difficult. But because I was young, days were quickening, provocative, and noisy with words. As Mewshaw described the dangers and the problems he experienced traveling and trying to travel, my past flickered. In a refugee camp, children showed me their wagons. The wagons were homemade, the wheels fashioned out of coat hangers and attached to cardboard boxes.

In *From Paris to Tahiti*, Sarah Turnbull received a letter from a friend saying, "Sooner or later we yearn for the one place we don't need to constantly explain ourselves." I have reached that place. Nova Scotia is calm and passionless. Now unless a writer like Mewshaw wanders a faraway that was once near, and dear, to me, I may start an account of rough travels, but I probably won't finish it. I've roamed the world with Paul Theroux since the appearance of *The Great Railway Bazaar* in 1975. I have ridden his pages to Angola, around the United Kingdom, across China, to Patagonia, and through the South Seas. This summer I stopped after reading two-thirds of *The Plain of Snakes*, his account of roaming the wild border between Mexico and the United States. I, not Theroux, had changed. He remains a fine and appealing writer, especially to people who greet mornings optimistically, seeing light even before opening their eyes. For me books are now electrical switches. They are therapeutic and flood rooms with artificial light. They invigorate and so dispel the shades that accompany age that one glances beyond the self and in the daylight suddenly notices the sky-blue berries of bay and the yellow rushlights of swamp candles. "The Mexican Border," Theroux began *The Plain of Snakes*, "is the edge of the known world, only shadows and danger beyond it, and lurking figures—hungry, criminal, predatory, fanged, fanatical enemies—a malevolent and unimaginable rabble eager to pounce on the unwary traveler." Good writing, but not easy for the elderly to digest, for people who totter and feel vulnerable whenever they climb or descend stairs, particularly not for the me who drives to D. J.'s Store almost every afternoon where Vicki and I split a piece of coconut cream pie, drink mild coffee, and talk about children to Lisanne, the owner's daughter.

Educators speculate endlessly about the influence of reading on the young and the comparatively wordless. They don't analyze its effects upon oldsters with the same intensity. I suspect reading shapes more learned articles than it does men or women. For most people, certainly those my age, if reading has an effect, it is individual. Near the end of my 81 days, I dreamed I walked across the United States from East to West.

I was careful, and the closest I came to Mexico was Iowa. My time in the nation's hog abattoir was not without excitement. In Des Moines, my Passepartout, a yellow cat, disappeared for three days. Eventually I found her, and we pushed on to California and our house, a red caboose on the land side of a bridge linking the United States to Stevenson's South Seas.

As usual during the 81 days I read a breakfront crammed with crime novels. This summer, however, I avoided body farms. I wasn't entirely successful. Unlike a mystery that is solved on the page and is summed up by "The End," living drifts into conclusions that are neither plotted nor satisfactory, and really don't conclude. For that matter much reading is happenstance. Some weeks I raced through the Yarmouth Library, grabbing comparatively new hardbacks indiscriminately, among them Michael Harvey's *The Third Rail* set in Chicago, a city host to more assassins than Ismaili state in the 12th and 13th centuries, and Alex Berenson's *The Counterfeit Agent*, this last practically a madman's mall filled with uranium, Glock 19s, and Heckler & Koch pistols.

For the most part I read old paperback mausoleums rarely containing more than two corpses, books by Agatha Christie and Ngaio Marsh for example. In previous summers I read Marsh's *Death and the Dancing Footman* and *Singing in the Shrouds*, but the titles appealed to me, and I reread the books. Several crime novels were in large print. I found these in the deactivation bin at the Yarmouth Library and purchased each for a dollar. "Mysteries for old eyes, guaranteed not to raise the blood pressure," Vicki said. I read many of the paperbacks sitting in our car outside Walmart while Vicki shopped inside. I didn't confine my parking lot reading to novels. At Bulk Barn, the initial stop on one shopping excursion, I bought a packet of Veggie Chips. Because their sell-by day was fast approaching, the chips had been marked down 75%, from $4.89 to $1.23. I planned to nibble while I read Iona Whishaw's *An Old, Cold Grave: A Lane Winslow Mystery*. I did not nibble long. One bite was enough. Veggie Chips was an appetite suppressor. Surprisingly, the back of their package was more to my taste than its contents. "News Flash," a story on the package began,

> five months ago a veteran wilderness expert disappeared during an expedition in the Alaskan wilderness. He gave a Juneau grocery market owner quite a surprise when he walked out of the woods into the store and immediately headed for the snack aisle. Later questioned by police, he claimed to have survived solely on the veggie snacks he had taken with him. Incidentally, he had lost his wallet in the wilderness and was arrested for shoplifting more veggie snacks.

Although the news flash satisfactorily explained the expert's survival, other mysteries appeared on the package. Listed among the ingredients of Veggie Chips were "No Artificial Flavours or Colours." Why did the British spelling of flavor and color appear on the container of a product, the package declared, "Made in America," distributed by a company in Folsom, California, and decorated with a small American flag?

I took breaks while reading in the car. I leaned across the driver's arm rest and stretched to prevent my legs from cramping. Occasionally I shifted from the front to the back seat. I stayed there a while then returned to the front. Often, I laid my book aside and looking out the window studied people pushing grocery carts across the asphalt. On Fridays they purchased carcasses of meat, cases of soda, massive shiny bags of edible chips, and bakeries of hot dog and hamburger buns. Many people wore readable shirts. Printed on them were discouraging statements like "Go To Church. But Trust A Shotgun," "Chickens, The Only Pets That Poop Breakfast," and "All I Care About Is My Dog." Few statements were interesting although many were vague, "If You Can't Find Yours, I'll Give You Mine," for example. I was disappointed that none were literary. In April, in South Carolina I saw a man sporting a tattoo featuring the old saying, "Tit For Tat. Butter Is Fat. You Kill My Dog. I'll Kill Your Cat."

A few passersby stared through the window at me. Because my Nova Scotia wardrobe is old enough to have been woven in a literate time, sometimes my shirts are ecologically readable. While a few are buggy, others are reptilian. On the front of one of my automotive armchair shirts was "Know Your Insects," a cartoon from The Far Side. Depicted were shoulder or head portraits of Doug, Linda, and Liz, among others. Liz was a praying mantis, Linda perhaps a cockroach, and Doug a no-neck beetle. On another shopping day, I wore a tree frog shirt. The Anurans were originally from South American rain forests. I don't know whether they arrived in North America and settled on my shirt as illegal or zoological migrants. In any case, ten frogs congregated in a home week circle on my chest. Although all the frogs were partly black, they were individuals, each distinguished by a medley of colors, splotches of blue and green, white dots, bands of red, and torpedo-like orange lines. Fifty years ago, I imagined reading in a musky keep surrounded by walls of leather-bound books. I sat in an upholstered Edwardian armchair. The chair was thick and deep, and I practically sank from sight, my feet jutting out, slippered, and resting on a footstool. On a side table next to me sat a sherry glass etched with Greek keys and filled with tawny port. Time bleaches fantasies. During the summer as I read at Walmart, I imagined that this was how life ended: sealed in a tinny sarcophagus, anonymous in a parking lot outside a Super Store, the surrounding air putrid with exhaust fumes, people digging like grubs into the trunks of cars, beside me a crumpled napkin and a soggy paper coffee cup from Tim Hortons. And what book was I holding—a big print discard of either Margaret *Erskine's Don't Look Behind You* or *Mortal Remains* by Margaret Yorke?

Words are pliant, and the breezes of time and place blow them about like phragmites. Consequently, meanings are supple and personal, and even the most scrupulous and conscientious use of words is inexact. Only the green, that is, the teachable, dig through books searching for the roots of things. At my age lessons vanish quicker than chalk from a blackboard. What fiction lingers in thought is not because it means or explains but because it provokes association. Unless forgetfulness harrows their minds, the longer people live the more memories they accumulate. Accordingly, the possibility that story will awaken recollection increases. Amid the stirring of nonfictional memories, however, a plot often disappears before "The End" caps its last page. During our 81 days, I read a publisher's clearing house of novels other than mysteries. In Kazuo Ishiguro's *The Buried Giant*, Axel and Beatrice, an elderly couple, lived on "the fringes of the warren," that is, the outskirts of community. Their room was cold and unlit. When they were young and had children, they lived close to the Great Chamber and the fire around which people gathered at night. Now the mist of forgetfulness obscured their past, and they wondered if they ever had children. For summer after summer, Vicki and I took our children with us to Nova Scotia. The house's being unheated didn't matter. Affection and the noisy bustle of doing warmed the rooms. The children explored backhouse and barn and roamed bog and wood. They opened trunks. Old clothes became the costumes of the famous dancing, singing combo "Spuds Bucket and Hands Rock and Roll." Forty years of cancelled checks from the Green Tree Inn owned by Vicki's grandmother in Hebron became Monopoly money then confetti. They played the Chute and Hall parlor organ and bugled sunrise with a battered trumpet. They rumpused about in the loft and in the woods threw mushrooms at each other. George, the almost dachshund, was their faithful companion running with them along the shoreline and plodding behind them across bogs. They caught snakes and dragonflies, named squirrels, and identified moths and caterpillars. They picked blueberries and wild strawberries and collected buckets of seashells and rocks.

Some mornings eiderdowns of fog covered the fields, but that never dampened our lives. Every night I told stories, and "lights out" never really meant lights out. I love and admire the adults our children have become. But I miss those children. Memory loss hasn't clouded my days, and I ache to hold the little them again. *The Buried Giant* brought the past so much to mind and heart that I almost envied Axel and Beatrice, confused in the fog of forgetfulness. "Damnation," I exclaimed one morning as I sat in the study reading. Shortly afterward I shrugged, shut the novel, and going into the backhouse grabbed a hoe and a heavy pair of shears. Then I walked across the side meadow and under the old willow began cutting away the rough grasses that covered the grave of George who died in 2004, a yesterday nineteen years ago.

Nonfiction writers quickly learn to eschew consistency. Unlike *The Buried Giant*, the two novels I enjoyed most during the summer did not cause me to reflect upon my actual life. Margery Sharp's *Cluny Brown* was a comedy, shattering the confining wainscotting of drab propriety. Cluny, the heroine of the novel, was a bright upstart. She, an admirer judged, didn't know her place. As a result, Cluny didn't comport herself as society demanded girls born to her station should behave. If I had met and kissed Cluny while roaming Britain fifty years ago, maybe I wouldn't have misspent decades mortaring one short declarative sentence atop another. Had lips led me astray what occurred next would have been short-lived and probably dishonorable. But so what, Cluny and I would have had fun. We'd have rolled out the barrel, shouted "huzzah," kicked up our heels, and let joy reign unconfined. "Toss the Ativan and Zolpidem out the window, and every night before burrowing under the covers swallow a dose of impossible Romance," my friend Josh advises, "and you'll sleep like a dream within a dream."

The second novel which delighted me was *Lady L.* Romain Gary's prose resembled the icing on a grocery store cake, embossed and adorned with plastic flowers and purple bonbons. It was so ornate that it was comically and enticingly decadent. In truth the book's floral decorations attracted me more than the narrative. Perhaps the gray appearance of Four Winds made me inordinately susceptible to artificiality. Certainly, the novel diverted attention from reality, and I stopped fretting about the ceilings which hung above my head sagging middle-aged and obese. For a day I ignored the plaster that fell from the walls and crumbling spread across the upstairs floors in white uric splatters. How nice to escape meaning and high seriousness and luxuriate in the consciously overwrought, a mood that gritty daily life abrades. "The window was open," the novel began full-lipped, almost lasciviously as if injected with Botox.

> The bouquet of tulips and roses, against the blue of the sky and the light summer air, reminded her of Matisse, and even the yellow petals falling on the window ledge seemed to arrange themselves gracefully for a master's brush. Lady L. hated yellow and she wondered how the flowers had found their way into the Ming vase.

Ming vase, indeed, rather different from a birthday fare of bar clams in Yarmouth, on the table packets of ketchup and commercial tartar sauce, and the aroma of French fries seasoning the restaurant and providing atmosphere.

Perception is the slavey of Time. I closed Gary's novel weeks ago and have since shed most of its seductive effects. Now, I suspect, nay know, that the roses browning by the kitchen meadow at Four Winds were more fragrant than the pick of Lady L.'s yellow roses. That latter-day actuality aside, however, Gary's book opened on Lady L.'s 80th birthday. In attendance were her family including her grandchildren and great-grandchildren whom she didn't like "particularly," most of whom "merely smelled of milk." Also present was her longtime devotee Sir Percy Rodiner, the Poet Laureate or Old Silly, as Lady L. and the world knew him. He "had managed to outlive all her other pets and there were times when she almost regretted it." To him, Lady L. told the stories of her life. Percy was so bland that he was incapable of being shocked. Generally, however, he was inert, a ludicrous bystander set in gilt prose. "Sir Percy was sitting there," Gary wrote, "his hands crossed over his walking stick. The two dark swans were gliding slowly between the water lilies. The air was sweet and insects were darting over the pond, among the trembling butterflies."

In a leisurely manner Gary traced Lady L.'s biography beginning with her birth in the Rue de Lappe as Annette Boudin, the daughter of a laundress mother and an alcoholic revolutionary and sometime agent provocateur father. At fifteen she became an entrepreneur marketing commercial affection. Because she was smart and pretty, she attracted benefactors. Like all lives shaped by paragraphs, hers was episodic, featuring spells of virulent anarchism, an obsessive love, travel, a new curried identity, a surprising pregnancy, and social mobility. Her greatest patron was the Duke of Glanville whom she married on his sickbed and who not only taught her the ways of art and the world but who also guaranteed her acceptance by society. The Duke had limitless means and could afford to be willful and offensive. He, Dicky to his friends, was intriguing especially to readers who early in life donned blinders. Doing so was self-serving, enabling such readers to ignore the temptations of talent and ambition, making living quietly and indulgently possible. In later years after shutting the novels of the moment, jotting down items to buy at Walmart, and with their spouses dividing the 710 calories and the 43 grams of fat in Wendy's "New Loaded Nacho Cheeseburger," they may have regretted not tossing the reins of inhibition and galloping wildly astray.

Dicky was in his sixties when Lady L. met him. "For years," Gary wrote,

> he had been Queen Victoria's pet aversion. His enemies considered him corrupt; his friends saw him as an embodiment of wisdom. His eccentricity was famous, an

> eccentricity that was his own peculiar form of revolt. He had probably inherited it from his father, who had accompanied Lord Byron on his ill-fated expedition to Greece, not, as he took care to explain, because he cared about Greek independence, but because he had always regretted that he had not been there to listen when Nero fiddled while Rome burned, and he was sure that in flaming Greece, Byron's fiddle would find some of its most beautiful harmonies.

"What a guy," Vicki said.

Lady L. was the last book I read during the summer. The end of September had arrived. Cinnamon ferns became bronze and brittle. The fruits of wild raisin blackened and turned sweet. Jewelweed lost its flowers, and blossoms on white-topped asters hung over soiled, looking like stuffing squeezed out of pillows. Blue jays suddenly started calling from the dead tree across the side meadow, and sparrows began gleaning the hawthorns. Crane flies and toadlets appeared in the grass. Hummingbirds abandoned feeders and flew South. Kestrels arrived, and feathers from flickers caught in weeds along the lane. Summer residents began flocking home, and D. J.'s and the Shore Grocery stopped selling ice cream. Vicki scrubbed the house, and I cleaned the barn. Before leaving, she contacted a roofer in hopes of plugging the leaks around the chimneys. Everything went as usual. Although the eighty-one days had been monotonous, they had been comfortable.

"If we are healthy enough to return next summer," Vicki asked, "what will you do? The flowers and birds are old acquaintances, and you've read every good book in the Yarmouth Library." "Maybe the children should visit," I said. "Maybe," she answered. "We are not young, and monotony is easier on the old than excitement." As Vicki closed the house, I thought of Helen Hunt Jackson's poem "September."

> The goldenrod is yellow; / The corn is turning brown; / The trees in apple orchards / With fruit are bending down," I recited. "From dewy lanes at morning / The grapes' sweet odors rise; / At noon the roads all flutter / With yellow butterflies."

"Nice but really romantic and not practical," Vicki said. "I know," I replied, "life doesn't flow quite so smoothly, and rarely are days ambrosial. At home stinkhorn mushrooms must be pushing through the compost around the boxwoods." "Isn't the stinkhorn one of your favorite mushrooms?" Vicki said. "You bet," I replied. "Doesn't it attract swarms of flies?" Vicki said. "Yes. Sulphur butterflies and Concord grapes are wondrous, but if dipterans, the gagging perfume of carrion, and all seemingly distasteful sensory things vanished, days would lose the exhilarating overbite of piquancy."

On arriving at the motel in Yarmouth where we planned to spend the night before catching *The Cat* in the morning, we learned that for the second year in a row our sailing had been cancelled. Early the next day, we hustled up to Digby and once again took the ferry to New Brunswick. From there we drove to Augusta, Maine, where we spent the night in a Comfort Inn. We ate dinner in a nearby restaurant. Our waitress was pleasant and good-natured. "It must be hard work to smile all day," I said to her. She nodded then said, "You have to eat shit a lot." "Today," she continued, "a woman hissed at me." When we got home the next afternoon, the telephone was ringing. Calling was Harsad P. Patel. I did not answer. "Patel Patel," Vicki said. "What a guy!"

9

Afterword

In *Joseph Andrews*, Henry Fielding said that statements introducing chapters in books resembled "Inscriptions over the Gates of Inns," preparing readers for the entertainment they could expect inside. Chapter titles themselves are also inscriptions. An Afterword is different. In this book it is the remnant of a gate, its hinges rusted, pickets broken, and posts leaning akimbo. The landscape beyond the gate isn't intoxicating. It is familiar and plain. No minstrel wanders by and plays a flageolet. No bard recites heroic verse. No bawds beckon from the Temple of Venus. In these final pages, I continue to live small. On "Dirty Fryday" when fried potatoes were free at Jefferson Fries in Storrs, Vicki and I had a home date. We bought Husky Hot Chicken sandwiches and ate them and a bag of taco fries in the study while watching *Miss Scarlet* on PBS. Some other Fryday, we'll purchase takeout again, this time when the fries of the day are milder, either Bacon-Cheese or Chicken-Curry.

Much that disquieted me on the lively side of the Afterword will continue to do so. Concerns don't vanish immediately. They just fade. On Saturday I read John Lane's *Coming Into Animal Presence*. In the book, Lane observed a goose on a pond near his house. Shot by a hunter, the goose was dying. Lane is an outdoorsman, but he doesn't hunt. As he studied the goose, he mused, asking, "How do we live in a world where everyone is not a hunter, and yet we buy our chicken from Publix?" Issues sometimes seem complex, but answers can be simple and direct especially from people who have aged into Afterwords and jettisoned temporizing mannered amenability. "I can't get past animal presences," Lane writes, "and the presence that is most disturbing to me is their dead presence." Neither can I. After reading Lane's book, I went for a walk. In the middle of Westwood lay an opossum, probably run over by a beery student speeding to a basketball game. I peeled the opossum off the asphalt, carried it into a wood, and buried it. A branch torn from a black birch by a high wind served as a tombstone while the funeral service featured a litany of language used in my house only in front of news programs or at the dinner table to describe the hedge-born.

Afterwords are often ashen and dry. They are not water gardens blooming with bees and honied dreams. How could Afterwords of people of a certain age be otherwise? The years of my closest acquaintances, as "Ecclesiastes" phrases it, have drawn nigh or damn close to it. "I spent the past week working on a gravestone for Betty and me," Harold emailed a fortnight ago. In February, an old friend wrote from a small town in Tennessee. She apologized for not sending a Christmas card explaining that she'd spent most of December and January in the hospital. Her single upbeat remark concerned the local funeral home that was "still providing sympathy." The same day I received her letter, an old classmate telephoned me. He rambled through two falls, a burglary, and the deaths of two wives from dementia. During the maunderings, his sentences tripped several times spilling vowels and consonants, so many that I soon realized that dementia had become a fixture in his life.

Beyond the gate, partings are not sweet sorrow. Neither are they bitter. They are simply endless. To escape the exhausting happiness of a family Christmas, Vicki and I decamped this year and cruised the Caribbean. While we were at sea, our seventeen-year-old dog Mee died. Mee was small, and the kennel where she boarded froze her body. The day after Vicki and I returned to Storrs, I dug a grave in the dog cemetery below my study window. We wrapped Mee in a shroud made from one of Vicki's work shirts and buried her during light snow. A dogless acquaintance questioned Mee's being frozen rather than cremated. Pickerings are more comfortable with ice than fire. Mee's end followed family tradition. Seventy years ago, my father froze Lula, his aunt. As Mee was a rescue dog, so Lula was a rescued relation. Her husband and only child had died, and we were her last remaining kin. Although she had long been distant, she was family, and when she began to suffer from dementia, Father shouldered her affairs and looked after her. Every year Father had a two-week vacation. When I was in high school, we drove to North Carolina and stayed in a cottage at Wrightsville Beach. For three successive summers, Lula became ill while we were away. Each time, Father cut his vacation short and hurried home to sit at her bedside. Lula survived the illnesses. Consequently, before leaving Nashville the next summer, Father arranged for an undertaker to freeze Lula if she died. Lula was accommodating. The undertaker put her on ice, and six weeks after we washed the sand and sun out of our hair, Lula was buried.

Final Afterwords are where books and scribblers collapse. More spaces than places, they are lumpy with the random, mulling whether to say, "presumptuous familiarity" or "the familiarity of presumption." Is "tooth doctor" preferable to "tooth dentist?" Should I describe the domestic haberdashery of a three-year-old grandson? Vicki's and my Sammy wears hats in and out of the house, and recently he has begun fitting a toilet plunger atop the head of Mikey, his one-year-old brother. Sammys are not and have never been boulevardiers. The top right-hand drawer of my desk is a wardrobe cluttered with notes describing low couture. The most recent refers to rammies, that is, trousers. Mine are so baggy that I can step in and out without disengaging the waist button. Every morning, I perch on the edge of the bed, slip my feet down the legs of the trousers, stand up, and tighten my belt. One day last week the belt appeared to have gone walkabout, and to buckle it I had to pull it back through the loops. As aged dressers will realize, I'd put my trousers on backwards, front to rear, rear to front. I didn't notice the sartorial mistake until after breakfast when I was in some hurry to find my fly and not discovering it caused an immodest inconvenience accompanied by unseemly colloquialisms.

Like the expansive roaming of youth, Time ends writing, not with a bang or a whimper, but silently in an Afterword. Two weekends ago, Vicki bought a three-dollar ticket in the Megabucks lottery. She won thirty dollars, her highest take ever, giving her a net profit of twenty-seven dollars. The following Monday I received royalties for the first year's sales of my most recent book. I pocketed fourteen dollars or "big ones," as Vicki called them, "half a large pepperoni pizza." To exceed Vicki's winnings, I'd have to write two more books. Accomplishing that would take at least a couple of years and who knows if the royalties would top twenty-seven dollars? Not only can I not bank on living that long, but I'm wobbly and lack the will to grab tines of pencils and rake through weeks piling up pages.

The seeping away of the need, perhaps compulsion, to write will undermine my curiosity. Not noticing "this" leads to missing "that." Intriguing things will occur, but I won't record them. My world and life will shrink. But that is okay. Diminishment is natural and restful. On Sunday Vicki and I trekked across Horsebarn Hill and ambled past the sheep and cow barns. Lambs were bleating, and we leaned over fences and watched young Morgans cavort and nicker. The air was rich and alluring, perfumed by the fragrances of sileage and manure. Pigeons settled on, then exploded off the roof of a silo, the flock shattering like pieces of a firecracker. Starlings whistled and chattered in the crown of an ash. I knew that trees would soon blossom, their flowers becoming, as a forgotten poet wrote, "the bright eyes of March."

In April, I'll see daffodils and violets. I'll sweep hickory shells off the front yard, and later I'll spread cedar shavings around the roots of boxwood. But I will not observe anything closely enough to transplant it onto a page. Life that does not appear on a page vanishes quickly. It's not remembered and in a sense isn't lived. A novelist once told me he wrote both to breathe vitality into his days and to make people interesting. "Off the page," he said, "people lack individuality and disappear into platitudes." Fifty years ago, I didn't agree with the novelist, but now I realize he was right. Nevertheless, I'll regret no longer reliving sweet moments. One day last spring Vicki and I sat on a wooden bench in the university rose garden. While we sipped coffee and nibbled pistachio muffins, the dogs dozed at our feet. Several students asked the names of our dogs after which they described their pets, named, as I recall, Parsley,

Patches, and Melinda. Among the passersby was a Chinese graduate student. She said she looked for us every day because we reminded her of her grandparents in Chengdu. "Like you they are old. I love them so much, and I miss them," she said. "Seeing you makes me less homesick." "Gee," Vicki said after the girl walked away.

Actually, this Afterword ought to be entitled "Endword." I've left the broken gate far behind, and I'm too old to retrace my steps. Fopdoodles, fustilugs, and raggabrashes don't interest me. Gossip about bedswervers bores me, and the only ware with which a procuress might seduce me is a cake, to be exact a devil's food cake iced with chocolate oozing flattery. But, of course, I will read. I won't roam afield hunting books. Instead, I'll explore the study. For years I've put books on the shelves and forgotten them. Only last week I discovered a leather-bound 1824 edition of Erasmus Darwin's *The Botanic Garden: A Poem in Two Parts; Containing the Economy of Vegetation and the Loves Of the Plants; with Philosophical Notes.* Thirty years ago, I purchased the volume in Yarmouth at the yearly "Buy Everything. Buy Anything" sale sponsored by the County Museum. Because the covers were loose and the spine fractured, I didn't pay the asking price of a dollar. I paid fifty cents. Erasmus Darwin was Charles Darwin's grandfather. Darwin was a mediocre poet, but he was extraordinarily learned, and the *Garden* was popular although later critics wondered how many, "if any," purchasers read the whole volume. The twentieth century bookman John Drinkwater opined that the work held "an extremely distinguished place among the best bad books in the language." I brought the book back to Storrs intending to read it. But its 4000 lines of verse and its massive mattress of sleep-inducing notes overwhelmed me. But now that I am practically a literatus of leisure, I will again attempt to read the book.

Among its oddities lurks eyelid-raising advice. Attached to a section entitled *The Temple of Nature; or, The Origin Of Society* is a lengthy note on "Hereditary Diseases." Darwin advocated mixing seeds from "different situations" to strengthen plants and protect them from disease. "As the sexual progeny of vegetables are thus less liable to hereditary diseases than the solitary progenies; so it is reasonable to conclude, that the sexual progenies of animals may be less liable to hereditary diseases, if the marriages are into different families, than if into the same family." "As many families," he concluded, "become gradually extinct by hereditary diseases, as by scrofula, consumption, epilepsy, mania, it is often hazardous to marry an heiress, as she is not infrequently the last of a diseased family." "Clearly the risk I took marrying you," I told Vicki; "was financial, not hereditary." "Enough," Vicki said, the word a command not a request.